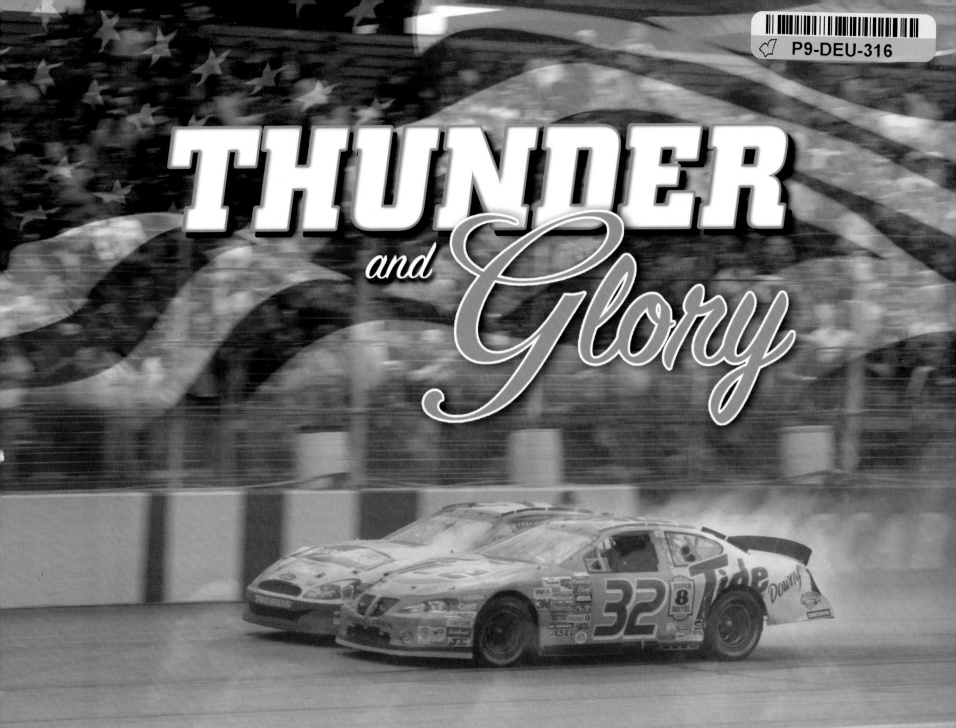

THUNDER
and Glory

The 25 Most Memorable Races
in NASCAR Winston Cup History

TRIUMPH
BOOKS
CHICAGO

This book is available in quantity at special discounts for
your group or organization. For further information, contact:

Triumph Books
601 South LaSalle Street
Suite 500
Chicago, Illinois 60605
(312) 939-3330
Fax (312) 663-3557

Printed in U.S.A.
ISBN 1-57243-677-8
Design by Valerie Deri Helvey
Title Page Photo by Bambi Mattila

Monster Memories

WELCOME TO *THUNDER & GLORY*:
THE 25 MOST MEMORABLE RACES IN NASCAR WINSTON CUP HISTORY.

Stock car racing is as American as apple pie and as deeply woven into the fabric of our culture as baseball or football.

When we decided to rank the most memorable races in Winston Cup history, we looked to another American staple, democracy, to guide our way. Race fans are as passionate about their favorite all-time races as they are about the drivers they follow. Ask five race fans about their favorite race, and you'll get five different answers.

In trying to rank the most memorable stock car races of all time, we first had to define our level of racing and time period.

We chose NASCAR's premier series and the Winston Cup era.

From 1972-2003 Winston Cup racing became America's fastest growing spectator sport. By the time Nextel stepped in as the series' sponsor for the 2004 season, NASCAR's top circuit was a multibillion-dollar international phenomenon.

Once we limited ourselves to Winston Cup era races, we were left to choose just 25 from the roughly 1,000 points and all-star events run from 1972-2003.

We assembled an expert panel (see chart), and asked each panelist to submit a list of what they viewed as the most memorable races in Winston Cup history. Once the surveys were returned and collated, the list of nominated races topped 80, with just three races appearing on EVERY survey. More than half the list only appeared on a single survey.

Taking only those races that made the cut with three or more experts, and using the number of votes received as our guide, the *NASCAR Scene* editorial staff undertook the arduous task of putting the Top 25 in order. Unable to limit the list to just 25, we chose to recognize five additional races as having earned honorable mention status.

With the ranking complete, we decided to offer readers a unique perspective on each race. Beginning with the original race coverage from *Scene* (except for two races from before *Scene* launched in 1978), and including a retrospective from Steve Waid on each race's place in history, we added many never-before published images and a foreword by NASCAR legend Richard Petty.

We hope you enjoy this look at the 25 most memorable races in Winston Cup history as much as we enjoyed putting it together. 🏁

Michael J. Fresina

Michael J. Fresina
Publisher – Executive Editor
Street & Smith's Specialty Publications

THE PANEL

Steve Waid – Vice President *NASCAR Scene* and *Illustrated*
Jeff Owens – Executive Editor *NASCAR Scene*
Jim Hunter – Vice President NASCAR
Rick Houston – Communications Director NASCAR
    Busch Series
Ben Blake – *Racer Magazine*
Godwin Kelly – *Daytona Beach News-Journal*, Contributing
    Writer *NASCAR Scene*
Mike Hembree – *The Greenville News*, Contributing Writer
    NASCAR Scene
Bob Moore – Former *Charlotte Observer* Writer
    – Freelancer
Tom Higgins – Former *Charlotte Observer* Writer
    – Freelancer
Tom Stinson – Street & Smith's *Sports Business Journal*
Art Weinstein – Managing Editor *NASCAR Scene*
Jim Duff – Special Projects Editor *NASCAR Scene*
Ben White – Senior Editor *NASCAR Illustrated*
Kenny Bruce, Mark Ashenfelter, Rea White,
Bob Pockrass – Associate Editors *NASCAR Scene*

CONTENTS

The King's Decree

"I wanted to go out in a

blaze of glory

but I just went out in a blaze."

When it comes to my career in NASCAR, I've been very fortunate. With the help of family members and a lot of good people, I've had many memorable experiences. I've been able to win 200 races and as far as I'm concerned, any race I won was a "great" race.

More than that, I have been privileged to be a part of NASCAR history.

That's what this book, "Thunder & Glory: The 25 Most Memorable Races in Winston Cup History" is all about. It's about the great races of the Winston Cup era, from 1972-2003.

I remember all of them. Fact is, I could never forget a lot of them because I was smack dab in the middle of 'em. The 1992 Hooters 500 at Atlanta Motor Speedway is memorable because it was my last start. OK, it didn't turn out the way I would have liked – I crashed and my car caught fire but I did come up with a good line, "I wanted to go out in a blaze of glory but I just went out in a blaze."

But more important than it being my last race, it turned out to be a real thriller. Alan Kulwicki finished second but won the Winston Cup championship by just 10 points over Bill Elliott, who won the race. That was the closest championship battle in Winston Cup history. Oh, and some kid named Jeff Gordon made his first start.

David Pearson and I had a heckuva battle in the 1976 Daytona 500. We crashed coming out of the fourth turn and if I could have just gotten my car started … well, he did and limped over the finish line. That was just one of the many times the ol' "Silver Fox" and I went at it.

Now, in 1979 in the Daytona 500, I was pretty much resigned to finishing third behind Cale Yarborough and Donnie Allison. But when those two scrappers crashed down the backstretch, the door was open for me. Hey, you take every opportunity you can to win in NASCAR.

But while I'm pleased to be a part of it, this book certainly isn't all about me. It's about the many great drivers who provided so many thrills. It's about races that were special and in many cases, became defining moments in the growth of NASCAR. It's about an era that should never be forgotten, with its good times and bad.

I'm a firm believer that while we all should look forward to the future, we should never forget the past. This book provides us the opportunity to revisit some of the best races in NASCAR's history and the drivers who made them so.

Like I said, I am very pleased to be a part of it all. More than that, I'm pleased that NASCAR fans have this opportunity to enjoy the experience of reading about the greatest races of an important era in NASCAR.

—Richard Petty

Elliott Rocks Atlanta Again; But Title Is Kulwicki's

Late-Race Drama Adds Spice To Storybook Season Finish

Perhaps no other NASCAR race had more storylines than this one. It was the final race for the legendary Richard Petty after 35 years of competition. It was the first for a kid named Jeff Gordon, who would soon usher in a new era, and it featured a tense battle for the championship. Maverick team owner/driver Alan Kulwicki used excellent strategy to lead one more lap than race winner Bill Elliott, the driver for Junior Johnson's powerful organization. As a result, Kulwicki won the title by 10 points - the closest finish in NASCAR history.

—Steve Waid

Bill Elliott reached a goal in the Hooters 500, but it was Alan Kulwicki who fulfilled a lifelong dream.

Elliott, driver of the Junior Johnson & Associates Ford, rebounded from some recent hard-luck performances to win the race – and thus record his fifth Winston Cup victory of the season – by 8.06 seconds over Kulwicki.

But Kulwicki, whose Winston Cup career began with a pickup truck, some equipment and very little money in 1986, parlayed his runnerup finish into the first national championship of his career. The native of Greenfield, Wisconsin, became the 10th different titleist since the drivers began pursuing the Winston Cup in 1971.

And he won the closest title battle since the current point system was installed in 1975. Kulwicki finished with 4,078 points, only 10 more than Elliott (4,068). The winning point total was the lowest since Rusty Wallace became champion in 1989 with 4,176 points.

For Kulwicki, the race marked the first time he had taken the points lead all season. It came at the most rewarding moment.

Both drivers' achievements were made in the final race of Richard Petty's career. "The King" of stock car racing brought to a close 35 years of competition with a 35th-place showing in his Petty Enterprises Pontiac. Petty completed 94 laps before being involved in a multicar crash, which engulfed his car in flames and sent him reeling out of the race.

"I went out in a blaze of glory, but it wasn't what I had in mind," said an uninjured Petty, who waved to the relieved and cheering crowd after he exited his battered car. "Make that

Elliott won the battle in Atlanta, taking the Hooters 500 checkered flag, but he lost the war. Kulwicki took the title by a single lap.

just a blaze. There wasn't any glory."

The car was repaired well enough for Petty to rejoin the race for one lap – 327 – of the 328-lap affair around the 1.522-mile track. After the race, he and wife Lynda were taken around the track in a pace truck for one final farewell.

Kulwicki, 37, had his own post-race parade. He made what he calls his "Polish Victory Lap," encircling the track in the wrong direction, after the checkered flag assured him the title was his. The last time Kulwicki made the lap came with his first career win at Phoenix International Raceway in 1988.

For four other challengers for the Winston Cup title, the day ended in disappointment.

Davey Allison, who came into the race as the points leader by a margin of 30 over Kulwicki and 40 over Elliott, saw his title hopes disappear in a race-ending crash with Ernie Irvan on the frontstretch on lap 253. He fell to a 27th-place finish and wound up third in the final tally with 4,015 points.

Harry Gant came into the race in fourth place in points and finished there, 123 points in arrears. He finished 13th in the race.

Kyle Petty's wounded Pontiac completed 320 laps and finished 16th, allowing Richard's son to wind up fifth in points with 3,945.

Engine failure in his Ford relegated Mark Martin, the sixth man in contention, to 32nd place. He finished sixth in points, 191 behind Kulwicki.

But certainly the contenders put on a show. Four of them led for a combined 257 of the 328 total laps.

In the end, laps led played a significant role in the championship outcome. It was Elliott, in his first year with Johnson's organization, who dominated early. By the time Kulwicki powered past him on lap 210, he had led 85 circuits to just two for his rival.

It meant Elliott had a firm grip on five extra

bonus points awarded for most laps led. When Kulwicki took the lead for only the third time in the race, he had to pile up laps if he wanted to eradicate Elliott's edge.

He did so, leading 101 consecutive circuits. When he made his last pit stop on lap 310 for a splash of fuel, he knew he had offset Elliott's only advantage and had the title won. Kulwicki led 103 laps; Elliott 102.

The race itself was another matter. Inheriting the lead after Kulwicki's pit stop, Elliott made his own fuel-only stop on lap 314. He came out with the lead still his, and that would not change.

"I did everything I could do," said Elliott. "I tried to lead the most laps, everything. I knew if Alan finished just one position behind me, he'd win the championship.

"They tried to tell me over the radio to lead every lap but that wasn't easy. With 30-35 laps on my tires, I thought my car ran better. Alan seemed to be quicker on the first 30 laps or so. The distance he'd put on me made it hard for me to catch him.

"When he pitted for gas at the end, I knew we were going to do the same thing. We had discussed under the last caution making a stop for gas only because we thought that would make the difference. Where we pitted (well toward the end of pit road) made a difference. When he pitted, he had to run slow down pit road, and then he'd have to go out slow.

"We could come in slow but then just go after the stop. We would keep the lead and keep him back a couple of seconds – and that's what we did," Elliott said.

Elliott's victory gave him a sweep of events at AMS, since he won the spring Motorcraft 500. It marked the second

time in his career he won both races at his "hometown" track, as he did it first in 1985.

"No doubt to win here in front of the hometown fans is special," said Elliott, who earned $93,600. "And it was different because we didn't back into it like we did here the last time. Our car ran good all day.

"It hurts a little bit to lose the championship, but it's no more bittersweet because of everything that happened. We ran good. We ran hard. We came here to win the last race of the year as well as the championship.

"If we didn't win the championship, we did win the race and because it was Richard Petty's last race, there's a lot of emotion involved. When they ask who won his last race, I can say, 'It's me.'"

The race was only two laps old when a spectacular accident crippled the efforts of first-time pole winner Rick Mast and sidelined number-two starter Brett Bodine. A crash between the two in the second turn instigated a seven-car mishap that battered Mast's Oldsmobile, put Bodine's Ford out of the race and sidelined Hut Stricklin's Ford as well.

Elliott with Hooters founder and chairman, Bob Brooks.
DAVID CHOBAT PHOTO

Other cars involved were those of Michael Waltrip, Rich Bickle, Wally Dallenbach Jr. and Jimmy Spencer.

Thereafter, Dale Earnhardt assumed control. He took the lead on the second lap and led all but 15 of the first 60 circuits. But he ultimately lost two laps when he ran out of gas on lap 61. He never made up the distance and was finally relegated to 26th place after he spun in the second turn on lap 203.

When Earnhardt ran out of gas, the lead turned over to Elliott for the first time. He, Kulwicki, Martin, Allison, Irvan and Geoff Bodine took turns at the point – with Elliott dominant – through lap 209. It was at that point Kulwicki took over and exercised the control that would lead him to the championship.

"Winning the race maybe isn't as good as winning the championship, but with what this team has gone through this year, we've accomplished a lot," said Elliott, who won four straight races in March and whose last win came March 29 in Darlington, S.C.

"When I look back on the season, we ran well all year, and maybe there were a couple of races we should have won but didn't for one reason or another," said Elliott, the 1988 Winston Cup champion. "But we had sort of an up-and-down year. It was a long year."

Typical of some of the "downs" encountered by Elliott and his team was the engine failure at Phoenix on Nov. 5 that plopped him from first to third in the point standings with a loss of 110 points.

"We knew what we had to do coming in, and we gave it our best shot," said Elliott, who has now won 39 times in his career. "To win here, to win five races and to finish second in the points in my first year with Junior Johnson – that's a lot.

"But I'm tired. It's been a long year, and I'm ready to get out of here."

Geoff Bodine finished third in the Bud Moore Engineering Ford while Spencer rallied to finish fourth in the Bobby Allison Motorsports Ford. Terry Labonte took fifth in the Hagan Racing Chevrolet while Rusty Wallace took sixth in the Penske Racing South Pontiac.

Rounding out the top 10 were Sterling Marlin, seventh in the Junior Johnson & Associates Ford, Jimmy Hensley, eighth in the Cale Yarborough Motorsports Ford, Ted Musgrave, ninth in the RaDiUs Motorsports Ford and Dale Jarrett, 10th in the Joe Gibbs Racing Chevrolet.

"I congratulate Alan," said Elliott. "He did what he had to do. And he came out on top. But we won this race, and I can't say enough about what all has been accomplished this year.

"To go out winners means a whole lot." 🏁

By Steve Waid

'It's Really A Dream Come True'

Kulwicki Achieves His Goal – And He Did It His Way

Alan Kulwicki said it to himself: He was a man not unlike fiction's Don Quixote; he was chasing the impossible dream.

At first, the vision wasn't complicated. He simply wanted to be a NASCAR Winston Cup driver. While he had admirable credentials – he was a successful campaigner in the Midwest, home of the tough American Speed Association circuit – he was not cut from the predominantly Southern stock car mold.

That meant he wasn't a "good ol' boy" blessed with ample sponsorship. Instead, he was an interloper chasing windmills.

Others may have thought that, but Kulwicki ignored them. He came to North Carolina in 1986 with a small amount of equipment, perhaps an even a smaller amount of sponsorship and struggled successfully on the Winston Cup tour. So successfully, in fact, that he was the circuit's rookie of the year that season.

But the dream remained unfulfilled.

"At first I just wanted to drive," said the 37-year-old Kulwicki. "Then after a couple of years, I wanted to win races."

He did so, first in 1988 and in every year – save for '89 – since.

"It was unrealistic for me to think of winning a championship at first," Kulwicki said. "I was just trying to swim for my life. Then after a couple of races, the idea of winning a championship stuck.

"But to get to that point took time. It took quite a while to build my team. We all had to grow and gain experience. Maybe that took longer, but maybe it will be better for the future.

"We came here with a chance to win the championship. We were going to do the best we could to win it. We were very close to it. We had come so close that even if we didn't win and finished second, third or fifth; we could still look back and say we had a great year.

"But being as close as we were, we had to capitalize on it if we could. To say you'll come back next year and do better may or may not happen."

Kulwicki seized the chance by leading 103 laps, just one more than Bill Elliott, the man he beat for the championship. Laps led made all the difference for the two drivers who dominated the Hooters 500. Elliott won, but Kulwicki's lap advantage was the key. Had Elliott won and led the most laps, the title would have been his for a second time.

But Kulwicki led 101 consecutive laps – laps 210-310 – and then pitted for gas only. That gave the lead to Elliott, a lead he would not surrender even after he also pitted for fuel, on lap 314 of the 328-lap race.

"I had been told by the guys I needed to lead until lap 310," Kulwicki said. "I knew then that even if I finished second, I would win the championship. All I wanted to do for the last laps was be smart and not do anything foolish. It would have been tough to lose the championship that way.

"All I tried to do was conserve. They came on the radio and told me to save gas, and I thought, 'What?' I just slowed down. It didn't matter to me to try to gain a couple of more seconds at the finish."

What Kulwicki has accomplished will be recorded as significant indeed, as he is the first man since Richard Petty, in 1979, to win as a driver and team owner. The fact is not lost on Kulwicki. As in the past, he spurned several offers to simply drive for other teams and rid himself of the responsibilities of ownership.

For example, only two years ago Junior Johnson, Elliott's team owner, asked him to become part of the organization many consider to be the best in NASCAR. Kulwicki refused.

He had his reasons. He sought to realize his dreams his own way. That meant seeing his efforts reach their conclusion, whatever that might be.

"I had offers to drive for other teams," Kulwicki said. "And when I didn't drive for what people say is the best, well, people said I was crazy. But perseverance, hard work and determination had helped me reach this point, and I know regardless of what happened, we would have a good year. I wanted to focus on that.

"It was a storybook ending. We beat that team, and one of the reasons was I stood so hard and fast on my decision to stand on my own."

It was a storybook ending in more ways that one. Kulwicki is sponsored by Hooters Restaurants, also the sponsor of the race. He won his first championship on the day of seven-time champion Richard Petty's last race.

"For those reasons, this is a special, memorable day for me," said Kulwicki. "It is one that I will always cherish."

Now, after becoming the first driver to win a championship without winning one of the final 10 races of the year, Kulwicki is charged with the responsibilities that come with a title. They won't be easy to meet.

Elliott himself said Kulwicki was due to experience changes in his professional life. Gone are the days when he could concentrate solely on racing and car preparation, something Elliott found difficult.

"That may be true," said Kulwicki. "That sort of thing seems to happen to others and it certainly happened to him. But I realize you can't be all things to all people all of the time. All I can do is my best to accommodate as many people as I can and try not to hurt the team.

"I want to keep things in focus and deal with things as they come."

Perhaps the fact that he has earned $1 million as champion will make it easier.

"The money is nice," he said. "I would be lying if I said money isn't important. But there is the prestige that comes with the championship. They can never take that away from you.

"If you were to bet money back in '86 that I'd be where I am today, you'd be as 'rich' as I am. The odds were slim. When you consider everything it took to get here from there, you'd say it couldn't be done.

"But you can't look at it that way. I didn't. 'Obstacles are what you see when you take your eyes off the goal line.' That's from Vince Lombardi."

The late famed coach of the NFL's Green Bay Packers, a man who never accepted quitting and believed in the rewards of hard work, would be very proud of Alan Kulwicki, indeed. 🏁

By Steve Waid

1992 Hooters 500 Top Ten

Finish	Start	No.	Driver	Team/Owner	Laps	Money
1	11	11	Bill Elliott	Junior Johnson	328	$93,600
2	14	7	Alan Kulwicki	AK Racing	328	56,000
3	8	15	Geoff Bodine	Bud Moore	328	32,400
4	18	12	Jimmy Spencer	Bobby Allison	328	27,000
5	6	94	Terry Labonte	Billy Hagan	328	22,235
6	15	2	Rusty Wallace	Roger Penske	328	20,100
7	12	22	Sterling Marlin	Junior Johnson	327	18,830
8	34	66	Jimmy Hensley	Cale Yarborough	326	15,300
9	22	55	Ted Musgrave	RaDiUs Motorsports	326	16,600
10	32	18	Dale Jarrett	Joe Gibbs Racing	326	16,950

Time of Race: 3 hours, 44 minutes, 20 seconds
Pole Winner: Rick Mast – 180.183 mph
Average Speed: 133.322 mph
Cautions: 7 for 45 laps
Margin of Victory: 8.06 seconds
Attendance: 162,500

Don't let the sun go down on me. Richard Petty returns to the track for a final Winston Cup lap to mark the end of his storied career.

DAVID CHOBAT PHOTO

2 Petty Backs Into Daytona 500
Victory Ends 45-Race Winless Streak

This was the first race televised flag to flag by network television (CBS). A huge snowstorm in the Northeast put people in their homes in front of their TVs, and they decided to check out this "NASCAR thing." They got an eyeful. On the last lap, race leaders Cale Yarborough and Donnie Allison beat and banged on each other and ultimately wrecked in the third turn, allowing Richard Petty to take the victory. There was more. Immediately after the race, Yarborough, Donnie Allison and Bobby Allison got into a scrap in the infield grass off the third turn. Viewers were thrilled, and NASCAR's popularity surged. Ah, the power of television.

—Steve Waid

They said no one would ever top the David Pearson-Richard Petty crashing, grinding finish in the 1976 Daytona 500.

The Winston Cup drivers not only topped it, but added some extra, totally unexpected fireworks Sunday in what was easily the most competitive and exciting Daytona 500 in the 21-year history of the race.

Petty, the slumping king of stock car racing, who was said to be racing against his doctor's wishes, backed into victory in the Daytona 500 after leaders Donnie Allison and Cale Yarborough crashed in the third turn about a mile away from the checkered flag.

To Petty and his legion of followers, the King was back on his throne much to the delight of an estimated 120,000 fans and a national television audience. The victory of about a car length over Darrell Waltrip ended the longest drought of Petty's career (45 races).

In posting his first GN win since the Firecracker 400 on July 4, 1977, here at Daytona International Speedway, Petty collected a record $73,500 from a purse of nearly $600,000, the largest in stock car racing history. Petty held the old record of $62,300 set for winning the 1977 World 600 at Charlotte Motor Speedway.

Petty, making his debut in an Oldsmobile with the familiar Petty blue and STP red, became the first driver to put an Olds in victory lane since his father, Lee, won the inaugural Daytona 500 in 1959 on the 2.5-mile trioval.

But Petty was not the man to beat on a gray afternoon with rain hovering over the track until the bitter end. In fact, a late morning rain delayed the start of the race by 10 minutes and the first 16 of the 200 laps were run under the yellow flag.

Buddy Baker, who won the pole, the pole sprint race and a 125-mile qualifying event, was the man to beat. But he never got into the race once the green flag fell. "It was skipping and fouled up on the first lap," Baker said after parking his Olds just 38 laps into the race.

Donnie Allison and Yarborough, both driving Oldsmobiles, which they qualified second and third behind Baker a week ago, and Bobby Allison brought out the second caution following an altercation in the second turn. All three drivers continued, but they were one to three laps behind – Donnie

There was exultation and relief in victory lane as Richard Petty celebrated the end of a 45-race winless streak.

DOZIER MOBLEY PHOTO

The Petty crew masterfully worked to keep their driver on the track and in contention.

DOZIER MOBLEY PHOTO

(one), Bobby (two) and Cale (three).

D. Allison and Yarborough were able to make up their deficits under numerous cautions. However, B. Allison never got in the right place at the right time to put his Thunderbird back in the lead lap.

There was a six-car accident about a fourth of the way through the race, and it took Pearson out of the event. It marked the third time in four years that Pearson has been innocently involved in an accident in this event.

The final caution appeared on the 139th lap. The drivers never made a pit stop under the green until there were less than 30 laps remaining. With 22 laps to go, D. Allison and Yarborough hooked up in a two-car draft and pulled away from the other contenders.

They were more than a lap ahead when they took the white flag signaling the last lap. As they started to go down the backstretch, Yarborough attempted to go under D. Allison, who took Yarborough down to the wet grass.

They tagged each other once, then again. They collided a third time and Yarborough cut his wheels

to the right and carried both of them up into the outer retaining barrier. They spun to the bottom of the track. D. Allison wound up fourth behind A.J. Foyt while Yarborough was fifth.

Meanwhile, Petty had gotten around Waltrip and Foyt, also in Oldsmobiles, for the third position. They thought that they were battling for third place. Petty was quickly informed to "stand on it," as the leaders were in an accident.

Waltrip tried to take Petty on the inside coming through the trioval, but Petty locked the door. Waltrip was on the apron with nowhere to go. He fell a car length short in a valiant attempt to post his first Daytona 500 victory.

When Petty took the victory lap around the track, he noticed the commotion in the third turn. He then went on to victory lane. It was an unprecedented sixth Daytona 500 win for him. The Petty team has now won eight of 21 Daytona 500's.

B. Allison stopped in the third turn after the final lap and he and Yarborough got into it. According to early reports, Yarborough cussed out D. Allison. Yarborough and B. Allison started fighting and a struggle ensued before it was finally broken up.

Despite the seven cautions for 57 laps, Petty still averaged 143.977 mph. Just before Allison and Yarborough crashed, they had turned a lap at more than 194 mph.

Thirty 22-car drafts were present throughout most of the first 250 miles. And as late as 375 miles there were still 10 cars in the lead draft.

Here, Petty passes rookie Dale Earnhardt.
DOZIER MOBLEY PHOTO

The race never got boring, as there were 36 lead changes among 12 drivers. It was the complete opposite of the twin 125-milers Thursday when it was strictly a parade-type race.

D. Allison led 91 laps. Benny Parsons, whose Olds began overheating late in the race, was next with 39 laps. Petty and Neil Bonnett led 12 laps each. The other eight leaders led nine laps or less.

Asked what his doctor thought now, Petty said, "You know how doctors are. The more you go, the more they make. Right now, physically speaking, I'm on top of the world."

And he was. His fans mobbed him after his post-race interview. He talked with the media for almost two hours. He first was greeted with a round of applause in the press box. The only other time that happened was when the unsponsored Parsons won the 1975 Daytona 500.

This was only the second Daytona 500 ever started under caution. The first was in 1963 when unheralded Tiny Lund won the race in a Cinderella story that will live as long as racing. The first 10 circuits of that event were under the yellow flag.

By Gene Granger

1979 Daytona 500 Top Ten

Finish	Start	No.	Driver	Team/Owner	Laps	Money
1	13	43	Richard Petty	Petty Enterprises	200	$73,500
2	4	88	Darrell Waltrip	DiGard	200	59,350
3	6	51	A.J. Foyt	Foyt Enterprises	200	38,550
4	2	1	Donnie Allison	Hoss Ellington	199	39,600
5	3	11	Cale Yarborough	Junior Johnson	199	34,525
6	33	30	Tighe Scott	Ballard Racing	199	24,550
7	28	68	Chuck Brown	Jim Testa	199	18,895
8	10	2	Dale Earnhardt	Rod Osterlund	199	22,845
9	37	14	Coo Coo Martin	Cunningham-Kelley	198	15,885
10	24	79	Frank Warren	Warren	197	17,475

Time of Race: 3 hours, 28 minutes, 22 seconds
Pole Winner: Buddy Baker – 196.049 mph
Average Speed: 143.977 mph
Cautions: 7 for 57 laps
Margin of Victory: 1 car length
Attendance: 120,000

Yarborough And The Allisons

Push Turns To Shove, Shove Turns To...

During the final lap of the Daytona 500, race leaders Donnie Allison and Cale Yarborough decided to have a 200-mph boxing match on the backstretch of the 2.5-mile Daytona International Speedway.

Several bumps, grinds, spins and crashes later, the two Oldsmobiles came to rest on the infield grass between turns three and four.

The speed slowed, but the action did not. Although the cars had stopped, the drivers contin-ued moving, with Bobby Allison joining the fracas which turned into a nationally televised brawl between Grand National champion Yarborough and the Allison brothers.

Generally, opinions were split as to whether D. Allison bumped Cale first, or whether Yarborough just ran out of track, but each driver blamed the other for starting the backstraight crash.

Although Yarborough accused Bobby Allison of blocking the track for Donnie, films show that he was not involved in the wreck. He did, however, drive around the track and stop in the third turn.

"I hit Bobby because he just smarted off," said a very angry Yarborough. "I knocked the hell out of him."

Yarborough continued by saying that the acci-dent and following incident "was the worst thing I have ever seen in racing. Bobby waited on us so he could block me off. It was evident. The films will show it. I had him beat."

"I knew how to win the race. My left wheels were over in the dirt and Donnie knocked me over in the dirt further. He carried me onto the grass. I started spinning and Donnie started spinning.

"Donnie denied doing it," added Yarborough. "Bobby pulled up over there, and I asked him why he did it. He bowed up and I swung at him."

"Naw, I didn't block them. I wasn't even close," said Bobby. "I rode up there after the race to make sure they were both OK."

B. Allison refused to comment any further, and security police were used to keep reporters away from his garage area.

When told what Yarborough said of the wreck and the fight, Donnie A. became fighting mad.

"I don't see any damned halo over his (Yarborough's) head. He was going to win the race, or else. I already knew what he was going to do, and I decided that if he was going to pass, it was going to be on the outside.

"He did the same thing to me in Atlanta (November 1977), and I was prepared for anything. When he tried to pass me low, he went off the track. He spun and hit me. He wasn't fixing to back off, and I wasn't fixing to back off. I paid my dues just like he did."

Donnie was asked if Bobby had blocked the track. "I don't think Bobby slowed down, and he didn't move anywhere. Bobby came up to see if we were all right (after the race).

"Here's Cale Yarborough and he walks over and punches Bobby while he's in his car. Pretty good sportsman, huh? He got out and called me a SOB and a rotten bastard."

Most reports were that Donnie never struck a blow to Yarborough, but what if he had been able to reach Cale?

"I'da beat his brains out, and I think he knows that," said Donnie A.

By Robb Griggs

Daytona International Speedway
Daytona Beach, Florida
February 18, 2001

3

Triumph Amid Tragedy

Earnhardt Dies At Daytona As Waltrip Claims First Victory

The first race broadcast by Fox Television via the multi billion-dollar network television deal brokered by NASCAR. As expected, millions tuned in. What they saw was an exciting finish in which Michael Waltrip edged out fellow DEI driver Dale Earnhardt Jr. to win his first career race. But as he took the checkered flag, Dale Earnhardt - the "Intimidator" who was unquestionably NASCAR's best-known and most popular driver - was involved in a hard crash in the fourth turn. It was solemnly announced later that he had lost his life. It was a stunning blow to the NASCAR world. For millions of fans, racing would never be the same.

—Steve Waid

Michael Waltrip's first Winston Cup victory was supposed to be a moment of supreme joy and triumph, a feel-good story to end all feel-good stories.

And as the final tense moments of the Daytona 500 wound down and it became apparent that Waltrip had a good chance of breaking his 0-for-462 non-winning streak, the 175,000 fans at Daytona International Speedway were all on their feet, passionately rooting home one of the sport's favorite underdogs.

But the triumph and elation of a spectacular day of racing ended horrifically. Just seconds before Waltrip crossed the finish line on lap 200 to claim the victory, seven-time NASCAR Winston Cup champion Dale Earnhardt was racing in close quarters with Sterling Marlin when he lost control of his Richard Childress Racing Chevrolet, veered violently toward the fourth-turn wall and was hit in the right side by Ken Schrader's onrushing car. Earnhardt's Chevrolet continued on, striking the wall at about a 45-degree angle.

Emergency medical personnel rushed to the bottom of the exit of turn four, where Earnhardt's stricken car came to rest. The unconscious driver was cut out of the car and was transported to Halifax Medical Center, where he was pronounced dead at 5:16 p.m. He was 49 years old. Doctors said an autopsy likely would be performed, but they suspected a basal skull fracture.

What should have been NASCAR's brightest day – a thrilling event, capping an extraordinary week of racing that included Dodge's return and Fox Television's first NASCAR events – instead turned into its darkest hour, an unspeakable moment of horror and the fourth time in nine months that a NASCAR driver lost his life.

The ironies were enormous: Waltrip's car was owned by Earnhardt, one of his closest friends. Earnhardt's son, Dale Jr., is Waltrip's teammate and finished behind him in the race.

It was the elder Earnhardt who last year vehemently criticized his fellow drivers for publicly airing their safety concerns following the deaths of Adam Petty and Kenny Irwin last year at New Hampshire.

"It's not ... a totally safe situation anywhere you race," Earnhardt said last September at Richmond. "I accepted that

In the closing laps it seemed Dale Earnhardt held the field at bay while DEI stablemates Waltrip and Dale Jr. battled for the top spot.

2001 Daytona 500 Top Ten

Finish	Start	No.	Driver	Team/Owner	Laps	Money
1	19	15	Michael Waltrip	DEI	200	$1,331,185
2	6	8	Dale Earnhardt Jr.	DEI	200	975,907
3	12	2	Rusty Wallace	Penske Racing South	200	676,224
4	30	28	Ricky Rudd	Robert Yates Racing	200	517,831
5	1	9	Bill Elliott	Evernham/Elliott	200	392,582
6	27	7	Mike Wallace	Ultra Motorsports	200	275,269
7	3	40	Sterling Marlin	Chip Ganassi Racing	200	262,354
8	35	55	Bobby Hamilton	Andy Petree Racing	200	189,259
9	38	12	Jeremy Mayfield	Penske Racing Ford	200	207,168
10	2	92	Stacy Compton	Melling Racing	200	168,770

Time of Race: 3 hours, 5 minutes, 26 seconds
Pole Winner: Bill Elliott – 183.565 mph
Average Speed: 161.783 mph
Cautions: 3 for 14 laps
Margin of Victory: 0.124 second
Attendance: 150,000

when I came into racing."

"Today NASCAR lost its greatest driver in the history of the sport," NASCAR Chairman Bill France said. "I lost a dear friend."

Until Earnhardt's crash, this year's Daytona 500 was shaping up to be one of the best in the history of the sport.

The new superspeedway aerodynamics package that NASCAR first adapted last October at Talladega produced some of the most competitive racing in years at Daytona.

Over the course of 200 laps, there were 49 lead changes among 14 drivers and a host of strong performances. Rookie Ron Hornaday went all the way from 42nd to third in just 14 laps, and the 10-car Dodge armada looked strong.

Marlin had the fastest car most of the day, his silver Intrepid R/T seemingly on track for victory in its maiden race until a flat tire under caution forced him to make an extra pit stop and dropped him to the back of the lead-lap pack.

Marlin and fellow Dodge driver Ward Burton led 92 of 200 laps of the Daytona 500 and seemed to move back to the front with ease, even when they got shuffled out of the lead draft.

But Burton's hopes at victory were dashed when he was hit by Robbie Gordon on the backstretch on lap 174, starting a 19-car chain-reaction crash that sent Tony Stewart airborne, and then rolling across the top of Gordon's car first, then teammate Bobby Labonte's. Stewart was examined at Halifax and released, suffering only minor injuries.

The massive pile-up brought out a red flag and set up a final 25-lap shootout for the win. Earnhardt Jr. and Marlin each led briefly after the track went green again on lap 180, but Waltrip took the lead for good on lap 184, driving the race of his life.

On several occasions, other drivers teamed up to try and slingshot around him, but he held the low line and the lead all the way to the checkered flag and his first victory.

Waltrip's win made he and brother Darrell the first siblings to capture the Daytona 500, and Michael's victory broke an 0-for-462 streak, making it the longest any Winston Cup driver has gone before winning his first race.

In interviews after the race, Waltrip was unaware of Earnhardt's accident, and his comments reflected the thrill of his first victory, not the sadness that fell on the speedway later.

"It was crazy. I couldn't believe the way it played out. I think that I really starting believing with five (laps) to go that I was going to win it," Waltrip said. "I had blocked off a couple of big advances behind me, so big that I thought Dale Jr. had my wheels off the ground once hitting me. And once I did that, I knew there were only a few more chances for them to pass me.

"I started believing I could do it and that probably made me more determined to use my head. My car just handled so well at the end that I didn't have to look out the window to drive it. I knew how it was going to drive, so I was looking in the mirror watching them and doing my job that way," he continued.

"It just all worked out perfectly. I couldn't even imagine how well it was going. We were able to hold off the advances of those guys and ended up winning. When I crossed the finish line I said to myself, 'This is the Daytona 500. Don't act like an idiot. It's just a race and you've won it. Cry now and have your stuff together when you get to victory lane.'"

Sadly, tragically, everyone would be crying a few minutes later. 🏁

By Tom Jensen

Prelude to tragedy.
BAMBI MATTILA PHOTO (3)

27

Last American Hero

Earnhardt's Skill, Toughness Made Him A Champion's Champion

His race car was a mangled mess, so crumpled that his fans couldn't believe he had just climbed out of it.

They were even more shocked when he climbed back in.

Jeff Gordon, his newest rival, was in victory lane, having just slipped by him to win the Daytona 500, denying him a victory in NASCAR's biggest race for the 19th straight year.

Yet there was Dale Earnhardt, standing on a tool box in the middle of the garage area at Daytona International Speedway, flashing his trademark grin, charming the media and holding court as only he could.

Earnhardt was by far NASCAR's biggest star, had been for years. Yet his myth and his legend had just taken another giant leap. Just when you figured he couldn't possibly do anything to expand the mystique and aura that surrounded him, he does the unthinkable, walking away from an ambulance ready to take him to a hospital and back to a race car that seemed battered beyond repair.

"We went bouncing off the walls and off the track, and we bounced right back," a smiling Earnhardt said.

A few feet away, his car owner, Richard Childress, was in tears. He was happy Earnhardt was alive, but stunned that yet another attempt to win NASCAR's biggest race had gotten away.

"That's the toughest man alive right there," Childress said, looking up at Earnhardt. "He deserves to win this race more than anybody ever has."

For the umpteenth time, Earnhardt had come close, challenging for the win in the closing laps of the 1997 Daytona 500 when all hell broke loose. He was in a fierce battle with young Gordon when he lost control of his famous black Chevy, tagged the outside wall and went tumbling down the frontstretch, flipping end over end in a crash frighteningly reminiscent of one that injured him just seven months earlier.

After climbing from his car and waving to the crowd, Earnhardt was taking the mandatory walk to the ambulance when he noticed his car was sitting upright, on all four wheels and with most of its parts and pieces still intact.

What he did next will go down as one of the most dramatic moments in NASCAR history.

Instead of climbing into the back of the ambulance and riding to the infield care center, Earnhardt walked over to his battered race car, fired it up and climbed back in, completing the final six laps in a car that would barely run.

"I looked back over and said, 'Man, the wheels ain't knocked off the car yet.' So I went back over and told the guy in the car to fire it up,'" Earnhardt recalled. "He hit the switch and it fired, and I said, 'Give me my car back.'

"I just wanted to get back in the race and try to make laps. We were running for a championship."

It was vintage Earnhardt, never giving up and doing things with a stock car most race car drivers never dreamed of. And he did it with a flare for the dramatic that attracted a legion of fans and helped NASCAR become one of the most popular sports in the world.

A year later, Earnhardt would finally capture NASCAR's crown jewel, winning the 1998 Daytona 500 in his 20th try and cementing his legacy as arguably the greatest NASCAR driver ever. It was his greatest triumph, but certainly not his last. He won five more races over the next two years and once again emerged as a championship contender, finishing second to Bobby Labonte in 2000 and establishing himself as a favorite to win a record eighth title in 2001.

Sadly, he never got the chance to fulfill his dream, losing his life in a crash on the final lap of the Feb. 18 Daytona 500.

Perhaps fittingly, he died doing what he loved best, racing for the lead at Daytona, where he had won more races (34) than any other driver, and the site of some of his greatest triumphs.

"I loved racing at Daytona," he said often. "There's just something about that track and that race that suits my style."

Fast, fearless and a ferocious competitor. That was Earnhardt, the man known by his fans and peers simply as "The Man in Black."

His death stunned a NASCAR community that

was still reeling from three on-track deaths in the last nine months. It was the seventh on-track death in the past 10 years. None, however, has ever been more shocking than the death of NASCAR's biggest star and a cultural icon.

"Dale Earnhardt was the greatest race car driver who ever lived," said two-time Grand National (now Winston Cup) champion Ned Jarrett. "He could do

him 76 races and seven Winston Cup titles, but earned him the nickname, "The Intimidator," a moniker he rode to much fame and glory.

"He was 'The Man,'" said Winston Cup driver Mike Wallace. "That sounds kind of silly to say, and a lot of people use it superficially, but it just fits him. He was 'The Man.'"

Kyle Petty, who grew up as the son of NASCAR's

A year later, his championship team fell apart, forcing Earnhardt to drive for three different teams. After a winless season in 1981, he joined Bud Moore's Ford team in '82 and won three races over the next two years.

In 1984, Earnhardt hooked up with former driver Richard Childress, beginning a relationship that would shape the future of the sport and form one of

things with a race car that no one else could. You never think anyone will get killed, but he was the last one you'd think that would happen to."

"Dale was the Michael Jordan of our sport," said Lowe's Motor Speedway President H.A. "Humpy" Wheeler, a close friend of Earnhardt's. "We always thought of Dale as being invincible, so when he didn't climb out of that car after the wreck, I knew it was bad."

Even after the shocking news had spread throughout the NASCAR community, Earnhardt's peers and rivals found it hard to believe.

"After the race was over, I heard things didn't look very good," driver Jeremy Mayfield said. "But, man, Earnhardt? You figure he'll bounce right back. Your first thought is, 'Hey, he'll probably come back next week at Rockingham and beat us all.'"

For many, Earnhardt, 49, was the epitome of stock car racing, slinging his ominous black Chevrolet around the track, bumping and banging his way to the front no matter where he raced or who he faced. His aggressive style not only won

"King," summed up the Earnhardt legacy this way: "For a lot of fans, Dale Earnhardt was what they thought about when they thought about NASCAR racing. He could do so much and was so talented. He knew it, and he knew you knew it. That grin of his, a lot of times you wouldn't know what he was thinking, but you thought you did. And it might not mean a thing in the world, but he knew you were trying to figure it out.

"He was the last cowboy."

Earnhardt's Winston Cup career began in 1979, when he won his first race at Bristol Motor Speedway and finished seventh in points to capture rookie of the year honors. Until the arrival of young stars like Davey Allison (1987), Gordon (1993), Tony Stewart (2000) and his own son, Dale Earnhardt Jr. (2001), no one had a bigger impact on the sport as a rookie.

The following year, he stunned the NASCAR world by winning five races and beating Cale Yarborough for the Winston Cup championship, becoming the only driver ever to win the title in his second season.

the most dominant teams in Winston Cup history.

Over the next three years, Earnhardt and Childress won 11 races and captured the 1986 title. In 1987, they had one of the most dominant seasons ever, winning 11 races, finishing second five times and capturing their second straight title.

After coming up short to rivals Bill Elliott and Rusty Wallace in 1988 and '89, Earnhardt returned to dominance in 1990, winning nine races and capturing his fourth series title, his third with Childress. Another titled followed in 1991, giving him more championships than everyone but Richard Petty.

A year later, Earnhardt suffered an uncharacteristic slump, falling out of the top 10 in points for the first time in 10 years following the retirement of crew chief Kirk Shelmerdine. While the late Alan Kulwicki won his only Winston Cup title, Earnhardt won just one race and slipped to 12th.

Not surprisingly, he and Richard Childress Racing returned with a vengeance in 1993. With new crew chief Andy Petree calling the shots,

Earnhardt won back-to-back titles again in '93-94, edging Wallace and Mark Martin both years.

The '94 title tied Earnhardt and Petty with seven championships each, putting him one shy of the all-time mark. The '94 season also signaled the arrival, however, of a new challenger to Earnhardt's throne.

A year after winning his first two races, Gordon shocked the NASCAR world by unseating

also involved in a string of uncharacteristic wrecks, leading to multiple injuries and causing many to wonder if he'd lost his edge.

While in the midst of another championship race, Earnhardt slammed into the outside wall at Talladega in '96, then tumbled upside-down on the straightaway, breaking his collarbone and cracking his sternum as car after car slammed

chance and do something to injure myself or take a chance and hurt someone else or endanger someone else's life."

A week later, he turned in one of the most courageous performances in recent Winston Cup history, withstanding incredible pain as he muscled his car around the 2.45-mile road course at Watkins Glen to win the pole for the Bud at The Glen.

Earnhardt and winning his first title in just his third year. He won a spirited battle despite constant ribbing from the driver 20 years his senior.

As Gordon began to win on a consistent basis, Earnhardt dubbed him "Wonder Boy." And when Gordon wrapped up the title, Earnhardt joked that "the kid" would probably drink milk at the annual Winston Cup Awards Banquet. Indeed, when Gordon accepted his championship trophy, he held up a glass of milk and had a memorable toast with the seven-time champ, a moment many believed signaled a passing of the torch.

The arrival of Gordon, who formed his own dominant team with Hendrick Motorsports and crew chief Ray Evernham, seemed to mark the end of Earnhardt's reign. He slipped to fourth in points in 1996, then went winless for the first time since '81 the following year.

To many, his struggles were the beginning of the end for NASCAR's biggest star. At age 45, Earnhardt began to lose the consistency that won him numerous races on tracks he used to dominate. He was

into his sliding machine.

Beaten and battered, he was not deterred. Two days after being released from a Birmingham hospital, he traveled to Indianapolis Motor Speedway for the Brickyard 400. Despite pain that would have hospitalized most men, he started the race he had won the year before and ran six green-flag laps before turning his car over to teammate Mike Skinner.

As he climbed from his car, he choked back tears during one of the most difficult moments of his career.

"Dadgum, it was hard to get out of that car," he said. "I mean, you know ... it's my life right there. I just hate to get out of that race car."

Though determined to race, Earnhardt gave in to the wisdom of doctors and his teammates, who urged him to give up his ride during one of the season's biggest races.

"My sternum is broke in two," he said. "If I would happen to get in another crash, it would put me even further back in my career as far as this championship run. I don't want to take a

"It hurts, but it's a good hurt," Earnhardt said to the amazement of his peers.

Two days later, he led 54 laps and finished sixth in one of the most grueling races of the year.

"I held on. That's about all I can say, I held on," he said as he favored his chest and shoulder after the race. "I felt good after that first little caution. I said, 'Well, heck, I can stand it.'"

"Dale is a determined person," Childress said. "Through pain and everything else, that's the reason he's the seven-time Winston Cup champion. He never gives up."

"Just tell him he can't do something," says his former crew chief Larry McReynolds. "Tell him he can't go to Watkins Glen and qualify with a broken sternum, or tell him he can't outrun you. That's all he needs to hear. All you've got to do is tell him he can't do something, and he will flat prove you wrong."

Six months later, Earnhardt would take his wild ride at Daytona, then get banged up again at Charlotte in May. Less than a year later, he took another wild spin, flipping upside down at

Talladega and singeing the hair off his face when Bill Elliott's car burst into flames.

"It singed my hair and burned my mustache up a little bit," he said. "I'll have to grow some new ones ... but I'll be all right."

Childress believes Earnhardt's injuries, beginning with the '96 crash at Talladega, contributed to his winless '97 season and his struggles in '98.

2000, silencing his critics with two of the most dramatic victories of the season and finishing second to Labonte in the championship race. In March, he nipped Labonte by inches in the closest finish of the season at Atlanta. Six months later, he added to his legend by charging from 18th to victory in the final six laps at Talladega. His second-place finish in the season finale vaulted him ahead of Jeff Burton

he said. "My eyes just watered up.") Tears not normally seen from one of the toughest men in sports.

After taking the checkered flag, his peers paid him one of NASCAR's most memorable tributes, lining up one-by-one on pit road to congratulate him on winning the Daytona 500. Earnhardt was moved and taken aback by the emotional response.

He admits that he should have held Earnhardt out of some races, but that's easier said than done, especially when you're dealing with "The Intimidator."

"I've driven race cars hurt, so I can understand," Childress said in June 1998. "You don't want to get out of your race car. I know how they feel inside. That's the reason I'm letting him drive hurt."

After winning the Daytona 500 in '98, Earnhardt fell into another miserable slump, scoring just four more top-five finishes the rest of the season and finishing eighth in points. Though he showed flashes of his former self the following year, winning three races, he finished just seventh in points, leading many to continue writing him off.

His competition knew better.

"He's still strong and his intensity level is there like it always has been," Gordon said prior to the 2000 season. "I won't count him out. I won't ever count Earnhardt out."

"Dale Earnhardt can still do it, and anyone that's ever doubted it made a big mistake," Childress said.

Predictably, Earnhardt came back strong in

and into second in the final standings.

When the 2000 season ended, Earnhardt was disappointed, but determined – as determined as ever to capture a record eighth title.

"I'm frustrated about letting the eighth championship slip away," he said. "But to think this is the only opportunity I'm going to have to win that eighth championship, I don't. I feel like I've got several opportunities, next year and the year after."

After his dramatic resurgence in 2000, no one doubted him, not anymore.

"When everyone was discussing whether he should retire or if he'd slipped a little bit, I think most of us on the race track knew that wasn't the case at all," 1999 champion Dale Jarrett said prior to the 2001 season. "I think you have to consider him a major factor in the championship battle."

Though he won seven Winston Cup titles, Earnhardt's most memorable moment came at Daytona in 1998, when he won the coveted race that had eluded him for 20 years. Afterward, he cried tears of joy. ("I don't think I really cried,"

"All the guys came up congratulating me, all of them wanting to shake my hand," he said. "There was Michael Waltrip, Rusty ... I had to go real slow or my arm would've gotten torn off.

"This win is for all the fans and all the people who told me, 'Dale, this is your year.' ... It was my time. That's all I can say."

Earnhardt's time ended three years later, seconds before his own driver and teammate, Michael Waltrip, won the 2001 Daytona 500. The legacy he left behind, the one he passed down to his son and drivers like Waltrip and teammate Steve Park, was summed up three days prior to his own Daytona 500 triumph.

"Any time you get the opportunity to win a race, you are going to win the race," he said. "I am never going to back off. I never want to run second. If I'm playing golf or baseball or running a foot race, playing cards or playing checkers, I want to win. I always want to win." 🏁

By Jeff Owens

4

Epic Battle

Craven Bumps And Bangs His Way To Victory In One Of The Closest Finishes ever.

Talk about great finishes - this one was the best. At crusty old Darlington Raceway, NASCAR's toughest track, drivers Ricky Craven and Kurt Busch went at it like a couple of desperate heavyweights. They swapped the lead several times in the closing laps, banging on each other all the way to the checkered flag and getting sideways repeatedly.

Surely they would wreck. Instead, they raced side by side to the finish line, rubbing metal. Craven crossed first, by mere inches, in a photo finish. It is regarded as the closest finish in NASCAR history and serves as a prime example of what stock car racing is all about.

—Steve Waid

Who expected this? Ricky Craven, NASCAR's Mr. Nice Guy, beating up on Winston Cup tough guy Kurt Busch. It's not surprising for Craven and Busch to make contact in the last laps of the Carolina Dodge Dealers 400.

But it's almost shocking that Craven banged and pushed back, locking against Busch – who'd lost hold of his steering wheel briefly – and refusing to back off in the last-lap showdown.

And that it was Craven who held on despite starting to spin. He ground his way past Busch at the line, taking the closest victory since electronic timing and scoring began in Winston Cup racing in 1993.

"That was the coolest finish I've ever seen and I'm glad I got to be a part of it," Busch said. "It was just an awesome duel between two guys."

And NASCAR is thinking of taking a race from this place?

Known for tough racing and stellar finishes, Darlington Raceway always seems to invite rough-and-tumble action. But on March 16 the track played host to an epic ending that left fans and drivers stunned and cheering.

Even the guys fighting for that top position.

"The last five laps were, I'm not sure," Craven said. "It's the most fun I've ever had in my life. You ride up and down the road and you sit on the couch and you think about these things. This is exactly what you dream of."

His wildest fantasies might not have included this close of a finish. Not even Craven knew for certain who had won when the race ended – until he saw his number appear on top of the scoring pylon. And still he wanted verification that the 0.002-second margin went in his favor.

Busch, who took the lead with a daring three-wide move on Jeff Gordon and Elliott Sadler, later leaned on, pushed against and generally battled hard against Craven to hold that edge.

His efforts were fruitless, though, as Craven showed unexpected mettle. He lunged, pushed and punched back. Shocking even his own fans, he managed to bruise past Busch for the win without creating ill will between the pair.

Not that he generally falls short of being a rough racer. But he's certainly never come close to smudging the line between

Nip and tuck. Ricky Craven and Kurt Busch gave fans an electrifying show to close the race.

BAMBI MATTILA PHOTO

Craven and Busch traded paint—and the lead—
several times on their historic dash to the finish.

BAMBI MATTILA PHOTO

aggression and going too far. Or maybe he just hasn't shown it.

"I have to confess to you that there are times when I get out that I wouldn't mind rolling around on the ground," Craven said with a slight laugh. "There are times that for a brief moment or two you just don't care."

This wasn't one of them. Teary on his radio after winning the gutsy showdown, Craven pointed to Darlington as the track where he most wanted to visit victory lane.

"This will be the greatest race of my life, there is no question," he later said.

That goes for many of the fans who witnessed it as well.

For the final three laps, Craven tried to push past Busch. He'd pull up to the leader on one end of the track and fall back on the other. He never managed to lead a lap at all – until the one that mattered most.

Busch blocked as much as he could and hit Craven with two laps to go. But their near-passes and nudges were child's play compared to the final-lap antics.

Never afraid to bump and grind his way to the finish, Busch has become known as a problematic guy on the final lap. Since tagging and passing Jimmy Spencer at Bristol almost a year ago, Busch has carried the reputation of an aggressive, hang-it-out driver when the race is on the line.

Who knew Craven could be the same?

"There are a lot of good rivalries out there," said Busch, who raced over to congratulate Craven in victory lane. "Ricky Craven and I surely don't have one. We've raced one another and given each other three or four feet every time."

Not this time.

Not that Busch played nice. Originally taking the lead with a breathtaking three-wide maneuver that left Sadler and Gordon in his mirror, he followed with a demonic dance with Craven.

Busch kept pulling away from the pack, seeming to have the race in hand until he lost his power steering. With 10 to go, Craven suddenly had a real shot at winning.

With seven to go, Craven cleared the last lapped car riding between himself and the leader. Cutting seconds off the gap, he climbed onto Busch's bumper for the final three laps.

And then things got interesting.

"It was kind of fun just to watch it," said third-place finisher Dave Blaney.

Craven crawled inside Busch, the two bumped in turn one and he briefly took the lead. But Busch bumped back and Craven lost the lead. Game over.

Not quite.

"I think I slid up a little bit and got a piece of him," Craven said. "Once I gathered my car up, I think he gave me a shot or he got in my right rear. Then all the sudden I found him in the front and I thought, 'How the hell did that happen?'"

With the white flag waving, Craven snaked back up on Busch's bumper. They moved high, they moved low, Busch blocking all the way to turn three before Craven cut inside and drew even. Coming off the final turn of the final lap, the two made contact.

"Coming to the line I had my foot on the floor as hard as I could and I tried to hold the wheel as straight as I could," Busch said. "He was running out of race track. I mean, the excitement level within the car, you have to block it out and you have to focus on what you have to do."

Craven didn't back off. Busch, fighting to hold onto his steering wheel, claims he couldn't move away from Craven's car. Craven, his back end starting to slide around, held firm and stayed locked with Busch's Ford.

"Let me tell you – we made contact from the exit of turn four all the way down to the start/finish line," Craven said, smiling broadly at the memory. "Once we got to the exit of four, that is when all hell broke loose. That's when we started getting together. I really don't know what it was like. I don't know if it was a good finish or not."

At the finish line, his Pontiac started to turn to the right in the beginning of a spin. Perhaps that's how

Craven's Tide crew erupts as their driver edges Busch.
BAMBI MATTILA PHOTO

Darrell Waltrip made a special trip to victory lane to congratulate Craven.

he picked up those millimeters in the photo finish. Perhaps that's how he finally won the race he coveted.

It doesn't matter. Winning is all that really counted in the end. And that certainly didn't come easy.

"I had to kind of talk myself into winning this race," Craven said. "There's so many ways to lose these things, but there's only one way to win them. And we just got fortunate today."

Or gritty. It's something he knows a lot about, fighting for himself.

Craven's endured some rough moments in his career. He's gained more than his share of headlines for a head injury that nearly ended his career and for team changes and numerous setbacks. He erased all that in one epic afternoon.

"My story is a little different than everyone else, but I really think that you need to experience that," he said. "It made me tougher and it made me better prepared. Although I would never ever volunteer to go through that again, I think that I probably got what I deserved or I had to have it happen because

it happened, and look at where I am."

Truly honest words from a compassionate man. Don't let that be misleading. Think this guy isn't as tough as anyone out there in Winston Cup racing? Think again.

In a season when passing has been virtually non-existent, Craven powered the sport to a new level. At a track where fans sometimes seem scarce, Craven heightened excitement another notch. In a race riding on the endangered list, Craven gave NASCAR a highlight reel that should last the season.

But Craven didn't think of all that.

He thought of what Darlington meant to him.

In 1992, when he first moved to Charlotte, Craven fell in love with the place. NASCAR legend David Pearson, the winningest driver at the historic track, took him around the place, offering such charming tidbits as, "Don't worry about hitting that wall. If you're up high enough, it won't hurt too bad."

Craven took the message to heart. His love of the track started on that day, played through his mind on this Sunday afternoon. He gave his all, wearing down both himself and Busch.

It was worth it. Winning in this fashion is something he'll treasure when he's old and gray, rocking on the porch at Moosehead Lake in his home state of Maine. And, perhaps, every day in between.

"The last three or four laps are kind of a blur," he said. "I'll be 65 years old, I'll be sitting on the porch with my wife and I'll tell this story 100,000 times about how we won. It'll probably be a thousandth of a second at that point."

By Steve Waid

2003 Carolina Dodge 400 Top Ten

Finish	Start	No.	Driver	Team/Owner	Laps	Money
1	31	32	Ricky Craven	PPI Motorsports	293	$172,150
2	6	97	Kurt Busch	Roush Racing	293	103,725
3	18	77	Dave Blaney	Jasper Motsports	293	91,945
4	27	6	Mark Martin	Roush Racing	293	114,813
5	9	15	Michael Waltrip	DEI	293	74,450
6	16	8	Dale Earnhardt Jr.	DEI	293	98,392
7	1	38	Elliott Sadler	Robert Yates Racing	293	94,470
8	12	17	Matt Kenseth	Roush Racing Ford	293	69,440
9	25	9	Bill Elliott	Evernham Motsports	293	86,743
10	28	20	Tony Stewart	Joe Gibbs Racing	293	103,158

Time of Race: 3 hours, 10 minutes, 16 seconds
Pole Winner: Elliott Sadler – 170.147 mph
Average Speed: 126.214 mph
Cautions: 7 for 33 laps
Margin of Victory: 0.002 second
Attendance: 75,000

As Craven celebrates the win, he knew he'd just made history—winning by .002-second.
BAMBI MATTILA PHOTO

At Last

Earnhardt Finally Bags The Big One

Throughout his career, Dale Earnhardt had won everything at Daytona - except the Daytona 500. He had tried for 20 years and said many times his career would not be complete unless he won NASCAR's most prestigious race. Again Earnhardt dominated the race, as he had done so many times in the past only to experience heart-breaking misfortune. This time, he held off furious attacks from Jeremy Mayfield, Rusty Wallace and Bobby Labonte as he raced to a tense finish, which came with one lap to go as the caution and white flags flew. Earnhardt got to the line first, and at last, the monkey was off his back. The grandstands erupted in cheers…and tears.

—Steve Waid

It evolved into a cloudy, gray day. But for Dale Earnhardt, it was the brightest of his career. Who needed the sun?

At last … at last.

In one of the most emotion-charged finishes in the history of Daytona, Earnhardt, a seven-time Winston Cup champion whose racing achievements are the stuff of dreams, did something he hadn't been able to do for 20 years.

He won the Daytona 500 – finally.

Now, as Earnhardt put it, "The monkey is off my back!" And he so exuberantly illustrated that fact by hurling a stuffed monkey across the press box.

With the victory, Earnhardt removed the one stigma of his celebrated career. No longer can it be said that Earnhardt, one of the greatest drivers in NASCAR history, can't win the Daytona 500.

And no longer will he be bothered by the question, "When will you win the Daytona 500?"

"Yes! Yes! Yes!" said an excited Earnhardt in victory lane. "Twenty years! Can you believe it!"

Believe it. After years in which Earnhardt lost the Daytona 500 in just about every way imaginable – out of gas here, a cut tire there, a missing lug nut over there – this time fate would not deny him.

Earnhardt, who has now won 31 races at Daytona including this first Daytona 500, also ended a 59-race losing streak and effectively hushed the talk that he could no longer drive 500 hard, competitive miles – talk that intensified after he mysteriously blacked out on the first lap of the Southern 500 at Darlington last year.

He was clearly the sentimental favorite in Daytona. Even those who do not count themselves among his fans said that if their chosen driver could not win, they wanted Earnhardt to win to end his years of futility.

And wouldn't victory for the long-suffering Earnhardt be a perfect fit for NASCAR's year-long 50th Anniversary celebration?

"This win is for all our fans and all the people who told me, 'Dale, this is your year,'" Earnhardt said. "I mean, you can't believe all the people who told me that, from the top to the bottom in the garage area. Team owners to crewmen. Bill France. Todd Parrott (Dale Jarrett's crew chief).

"There was a lot of hard work that went into this and I have to thank every member of the Richard Childress Racing team.

I have had a lot of great fans and people behind me all through the years and I just can't thank them enough.

"The Daytona 500 is over. And we won it! We won it!"

But he very easily could have lost it – again – and if he had, it would have gone down as one of the most disappointing episodes of his career.

As it turned out, Earnhardt held off a furious attack from the likes of Jeremy Mayfield, Rusty Wallace and Bobby Labonte as the 200-lap race around the 2.5-mile Daytona track sped to its conclusion.

Earnhardt, in a Chevrolet, was the race's dominant figure. But as he himself will tell you, that's never been enough in itself for him to win the Daytona 500. This time, it was.

Earnhardt, who led five times for 107 laps, more than any other driver, made a pass around teammate Mike Skinner on lap 140 to take the lead he would hold for the remainder of the race, although he certainly didn't know it at the time.

On lap 174, the race's second caution period began after Robert Pressley and John Andretti spun down the backstretch. One lap later, Earnhardt led the parade of leaders down pit road.

It was obvious that this would be the final stop and the leaders opted to make it as quick as possible. With the exception of Ernie Irvan, all took on right side tires only.

"We had learned from the 125-mile qualifying race that track position was very important," said Larry McReynolds, Earnhardt's crew chief who had won Daytona 500s in 1992 with Davey Allison and in 1996 with Jarrett. "We knew what all the other teams were thinking and to us, there was no question to go for just two tires. In fact, Goodyear brought such a good tire here we might have been OK if we just took gas.

"We knew it would take five or six seconds to take fuel and the guys made about an 8.5-second stop for tires and that let us get back out on the track first."

"On the last stop, I was focused," Earnhardt said. "I wanted to make sure I didn't do anything wrong and that we got out quick. And we did."

Earnhardt was followed by Skinner, Mayfield, Wallace and Jeff Gordon, the winner of the 1997 Daytona 500.

When the race restarted, there were just 12 laps to go. Earnhardt was in front with teammate Skinner behind him. That gave Earnhardt the ideal drafting partner and he would need it, because in third and fourth were Mayfield and Wallace, who became teammates in the Penske organization this season when Roger Penske became a partner with Michael Kranefuss on Mayfield's team.

It was clear Earnhardt and Skinner would combine their forces to escape Mayfield and Wallace, if they could.

"Mike did help a tremendous amount on that last restart," Earnhardt said. "I know he would have liked to have won this race as much as me."

But the strategy was doomed. On lap 179, Skinner was pushed high out of the draft in turn one and that allowed Mayfield and Wallace, in Fords, to close on Earnhardt's rear bumper. Gordon moved to fourth place and Skinner fought Labonte for fifth.

Five laps passed as Earnhardt, now on his own, eyed his rearview mirror and kept his foot in the throttle as the Penske Fords lurked just behind.

"I felt like I could do pretty good, but Jeremy and Rusty were hooked up good," Earnhardt said. "I don't know, but I just felt like this was it."

On lap 184, Gordon shot to the low side of Wallace in the first turn, but Wallace made a blocking move that broke his effort with Mayfield and allowed Earnhardt some precious space.

On lap 194, Gordon made another move. This time he went to the high side of the Fords ahead of him and split them, moving into third place behind Mayfield.

The running order stayed that way until lap 197, when Wallace shot by Gordon on the backstretch and once again united with his teammate.

Then, one lap later, pole-winner Labonte pushed his Pontiac to the high side and managed to clear Mayfield coming out of the fourth turn to move into second place. As he did so, Gordon drifted back out of the melee, the victim of a dropped cylinder.

There were two laps remaining.

On lap 199, the race's third and final caution period began when Andretti, Lake Speed and Jimmy Spencer tangled on the backstretch. When the leaders got back to the line, they would see the yellow and white flags fly simultaneously.

The first one to the flags would win the race.

Earnhardt gave it all he had. He was able to utilize the lapped Ford of Rick Mast as a pick and got a bit of a break as Labonte and Mayfield jostled each other for position.

Earnhardt glued a lucky penny to his dash before the 500.

He crossed the line ahead of them. And the grandstands erupted.

One last, comfortable, tension-free lap was all Earnhardt had left to make. With the checkered flag came the end of 19 years of frustration.

"We worked awful hard and just kept playing our cards," said Earnhardt, 46. "They'd go this way and I'd go with them or do what I thought was best. The years of experience helped me out there.

"I was hoping they would stay in line with about 10 to go or eight to go. It got down to five and they got to racing. They started dicing and that made me feel better. I could pick who I wanted to dice with as they were passing each other.

"When Bobby got in behind me, he was pretty much by himself. He didn't have any help. And we had Rick's lapped car there. I felt like I could hold him off."

Earnhardt admitted he got emotional as he sped past the yellow and white flags.

"My eyes watered up in the race car," he said. "I don't think I really cried. My eyes just watered up on that lap to take the checkered. I knew I was going to win it then, no matter what. I knew I was going to win unless something happened to the car.

"I was driving slow down the backstretch and I said, 'I want to go fast. I don't want to go slow. I want to get back around there.' I took off, came back around, took the checkered and really got excited."

By his own admission, what happened next will be forever etched in Earnhardt's memory. As he made his way down pit road toward victory lane, he was met by crew members from virtually every team in the Daytona 500, all of whom wanted to congratulate him for his victory.

"I sorta expected a few of them to come out there, but not as many as there were," Earnhardt said. "All the guys came up congratulating me, all of them wanting to shake my hand or give me high-fives,

thumbs-up. There was Michael Waltrip, Rusty ... I had to go real slow or my arm would've gotten torn off."

As if to display his excitement to the fans, Earnhardt sped off pit road, into the grass and cut doughnuts with his spinning tires. Later, fans would retrieve chunks of the torn-up sod for souvenirs.

The victory was worth $1,059,105 to Earnhardt and marked the first time in Winston Cup racing the winner's share of the purse was over $1 million. He won with an average speed of 172.712 mph, the third-fastest race in Daytona 500 history.

"I had confidence in myself, the team and everybody," Earnhardt said. "People say, 'Did you hear things? Did you wonder who was going to pass?' I was working to keep the race car out in front. I was working to do that until somebody turned me over or we got to the finish.

"I wasn't thinking about what could happen. I was thinking about what I was doing and focused on what I had to do."

Labonte wound up second, Mayfield third and Ken Schrader, broken sternum and all, came home fourth. Wallace was fifth, with Ernie Irvan sixth, Chad Little seventh, Skinner eighth, Michael Waltrip ninth and Bill Elliott 10th.

Earnhardt now is eligible for a $1 million bonus from Winston in the No Bull 5 program. He joined the other top-five finishers, Labonte, Mayfield, Schrader and Wallace, as candidates for the reward if any one of them can win the Coca-Cola 600 at Charlotte on May 24.

While Earnhardt would be the first to tell you he wouldn't turn

down a $1 million bonus, he's out for greater rewards.

"Another championship is going to make it complete," he said. "Honestly, I'm telling you this and not because we won the race, but because we've got a race team. We have guys who are ready to win races. We are going to concentrate on winning the eighth championship."

And now, there is no longer any need to concentrate on that first Daytona 500 win after coming so excruciatingly close over the years. Earnhardt ran out of gas to lose to Geoff Bodine in 1986. Then there was the now-famous cut tire on the last lap in 1990 that passed the win to Derrike Cope. Three times in the last five years he has finished second.

Today, he was second to no one.

"It was my time," Earnhardt said. "That's all I can say. I've been passed here. I've run out of gas. I've been cut down with a tire. I've done it all.

"I wrote the book and this is the last chapter in this book. I'm going to start a new book next year. It's over with.

"Every which way you can lose it, I've lost it. Now I've won it and I don't care how I won it. We won it."

At last. 🏁

By Steve Waid

1998 Daytona 500 Top Ten

Finish	Start	No.	Driver	Team/Owner	Laps	Money
1	4	3	Dale Earnhardt	RCR Enterprises	200	$1,059,105
2	1	18	Bobby Labonte	Joe Gibbs Racing	200	548,555
3	13	12	Jeremy Mayfield	Penske-Kranefuss	200	375,005
4	31	33	Ken Schrader	Andy Petree Racing	200	312,780
5	12	2	Rusty Wallace	Penske Racing South	200	232,005
6	10	36	Ernie Irvan	MB2 Motorsports	200	204,500
7	21	97	Chad Little	Roush Racing	200	126,980
8	8	31	Mike Skinner	RCR Enterprises	200	135,005
9	6	21	Michael Waltrip	Wood Brothers	200	142,005
10	19	94	Bill Elliott	Bill Elliott Racing	200	128,455

Time of Race: 2 hours, 54 minutes, 0 seconds
Pole Winner: Bobby Labonte — 192.415 mph
Average Speed: 172.712 mph
Cautions: 3 for 9 laps
Margin of Victory: under caution
Attendance: 150,000

A victory lap long overdue.

NS ARCHIVE PHOTO

Clash Of The Titans

David Pearson Emerges From A Wreck To Beat Richard Petty

Giants of NASCAR during the '70s, David Pearson and Richard Petty, were the acknowledged masters of Daytona International Speedway. They battled each other all day with the issue still in doubt as the last lap began. In turn three, Pearson slipped by Petty, but Petty quickly drew back alongside his rival. Then in turn four, they got together and slammed the outside wall. Pearson's car came to a halt at the entrance to pit road. Petty stalled in the infield grass near the finish line. Pearson kept his engine running and limped through the grass and took the checkered flag as Petty's crew desperately pushed his battered car to get it restarted. The race has a special place in NASCAR lore.

—Steve Waid

Richard Petty picked a fine time to get an ulcer.

Here it was two weeks before the 1976 Daytona 500, an appearance on ABC's "Wide World of Sports" hanging in the balance, and he was laid up in a hospital, his stomach burning like a forest fire from the pressures of big-time stock car racing.

Petty might have stayed there had he known what was coming.

Two weeks later, he would swallow his pride and choke down one of the most bitter disappointments of his career.

"I had one ulcer before the race. Now I've got two," he said.

Nothing can give a fast driver an ulcer quicker than a race car that won't start. And what worse time to have a stalled car than on the last lap of the "Great American Race?"

Yet, there Petty sat, his famous No. 43 Dodge sputtering and spewing smoke, his engine dead.

What was Petty, a five-time winner of the prestigious Daytona 500, thinking?

"Well, I wasn't exactly hollering, 'Hooray for me,'" he said.

To make matters worse, there was David Pearson, the old Silver Fox himself, sitting a few feet away, his engine still running and the checkered flag within sight.

The two long-time rivals had crashed – or wrecked each other – while racing for the win in the final turn. Now their crumpled cars sat in the frontstretch grass, one stalled, the other barely running.

A wild, dramatic showdown, one of the greatest in NASCAR history, was going to come down to which legendary driver could get his car started.

"Pearson won because he got his car cranked. I never could get mine cranked," the disappointed Petty said.

There may have been better finishes in NASCAR history. The fender-banging duel between Ricky Craven and Kurt Busch at Darlington in 2003, the closest in NASCAR history, comes to mind. Maybe Ron Bouchard's three-wide victory at Talladega in 1981, or possibly Dale Earnhardt's dramatic charge during the final laps at Talladega in 2000.

But certainly there has never been a more dramatic finish.

Petty and Pearson, two titans of their time, came out of turn four side by side, just like Craven and Busch and just like many others over the years.

David Pearson managed to keep his mangled car running long enough to win the race and get to victory lane.

DOZIER MOBLEY PHOTO

After his last-lap crash with Pearson, Petty was unable to get his hobbled car started as it came to rest in the infield.

But what happened next hasn't happened since, and probably never will.

Petty and Pearson, who had battled for the win at Daytona for the previous three years, were the only two drivers left on the lead lap, setting up a showdown that had the crowd of 125,000 on their feet.

The King, driving his family-owned, Petty-blue Dodge, and the Silver Fox, driving the famed No. 21 Wood Brothers Mercury, had dominated the race, swapping the lead three times over the final 46 laps.

Petty took the lead with 13 laps to go, but Pearson stayed tucked in his draft, sizing up his prey, preparing for the era's most famous move – the slingshot.

Petty knew it was coming, he just didn't know when. Finally, on the last lap, Pearson made his move, diving to the inside of Petty in turn three.

For a moment, it looked as if Pearson would surely win his first Daytona 500, denying Petty a sixth.

But then suddenly Pearson's car drifted high, opening a lane for Petty to retake the lead.

As Petty pulled to the inside of Pearson, Petty's car broke loose, Pearson bobbled, and both drivers went spinning and crashing into the wall.

"He went beneath me, and his car broke loose," Pearson said after the race. "I got into the wall and came off and hit him. That's what started all the spinning."

They were not the first two drivers to crash while battling for the win on the final lap and certainly not the last. But the drama was just beginning.

As smoke billowed down the frontstretch, tires squealing, metal crunching, two speeding cars spinning, Pearson's Wood Brothers crew yelled over his radio, "There's a wreck off turn four."

"Yeah, I know," Pearson said. "I'm in it."

The wreck was not over with their collision into

the wall, and neither was the race.

Pearson's car twirled around and hit Joe Frasson's Chevrolet at the entrance to pit road. Petty, meanwhile, fishtailed down the track before darting up into the wall. After spinning again, it came to a stop in the infield grass, 100 feet from the finish line, the engine dead.

"I didn't do anything to keep it from stalling, I just locked the brakes," Petty said.

Pearson, though, had the presence of mind to engage his clutch, keeping his engine running as it came to a stop.

"My engine never died because I popped the clutch," Pearson said. "I revved the engine as high as I could to keep it from stalling."

While Petty tried frantically to refire his engine, Pearson jammed his damaged car back into gear and quickly radioed his crew, inquiring whether or not Petty had crossed the finish line.

"When they told me no, I took off as hard as I could, which wasn't very hard at all," Pearson said.

With Petty stalled ahead of him, Pearson began to slowly creep through the grass, toward the finish

line. The checkered flag seemed miles away, and it seemed like an eternity to get there.

But as Pearson crept closer, finally passing Petty, his determination grew.

"If we had backed across the line, it would have been OK," he said.

Petty, meanwhile, was helpless. He watched hopelessly as Pearson took the checkered flag, winning the Daytona 500.

Finally, Petty's crew rushed to his rescue, pushing his stalled car across the finish line, a move that is against the rules and cost him a one-lap penalty. Still, he and Pearson were so far ahead of the field at the time, he finished second, on the same lap as third-place Benny Parsons.

As he headed toward victory lane, Pearson was approached by Petty's crew, some of them angry, others simply bewildered.

"I don't think Maurice [Richard's brother] was mad at me," Pearson said. "I think he was just trying to ask me what happened. But another member of the crew said some nasty words."

Pearson didn't have time to be angry. He was

Petty's in the lead—as he was often.

DOZIER MOBLEY PHOTO

Pearson takes the lead from Petty early in the race.

getting ready to celebrate one of the most bizarre and dramatic victories in NASCAR history.

Fans and the media, meanwhile, were going wild, not believing what their eyes were seeing. Action in the Daytona press box was as frantic as on the track.

"Guys were standing on the long shelves that served as desks. A typewriter hit the floor," wrote Steve Waid, who covered the bizarre event for the Roanoke Times. "Some were shouting as Pearson crept toward the finish line while Petty strained to restart his engine.

"Everyone was trying to see as much as possible to gather all the information they could. There were no TV monitors, no replays, no scanners, no radio communication with observers along pit road. It was a simpler time."

Simple, yet thrilling, the way many races between Petty and Pearson were.

Petty, ever the gentleman, initially took the blame for the dramatic crash.

"My car broke loose. The first time we hit it was my fault," he said. "I told David I was sorry. I didn't want my boys to get mad at him. If there was anybody to blame, it was me."

But after watching television replays, Petty wasn't so sure.

"You know, I think we were in control when we went through the fourth turn. Then David tapped me and that started me spinning," he said.

It was a finish the media had a field day with, calling it "spectacular" and "a classic."

Speedweeks had already grabbed national headlines with four top qualifiers – Darrell Waltrip, A.J. Foyt, Dave Marcis and Bruce Hill – getting disqualified. Waltrip, Foyt and Hill were accused of using nitrous oxide, or "laughing gas," to give them an extra burst of horsepower, prompting newspaper headlines to carry the word NASCAR hated most – "cheating."

While crew chiefs and team owners vehemently denied the charges, Darrell Waltrip stunned NASCAR and the media by admitting that cheating was rampant in the sport.

"If you don't cheat," Waltrip said, "you look like an idiot. If you do it and don't get caught, you look like a hero. If you do it and get caught, you look like a dope. Put me in the category where I belong."

NASCAR President Bill France Jr. didn't take kindly to Waltrip's admission.

"We only know what we find," he said. "We don't operate on hearsay. It's easy for others to sit around and talk like that, but we go only on facts. We always try to run inspections to the best of our ability. It's just that some days there's a little more controversy than others."

What NASCAR needed to squelch the criticism and controversy was a dramatic finish in its biggest race.

It got the gut-wrenching culmination from its two biggest stars – Petty and Pearson. They produced a finish that grabbed even bigger headlines across the country.

"What was supposed to be a great race on asphalt ended with a wild finish on dirt, like a half-mile bull ring," wrote Fred Seeley of the Jacksonville Times-Union.

"It was magnificent, heart-stopping and just a shade ridiculous," wrote Tim Carlson of the Daytona Beach News-Journal.

And Frank Blunk of The New York Times simply asked, "What can they do to top that?"

The answer was, not much. Petty would win the Daytona 500 again in 1979, taking another classic battle while Cale Yarborough and the Allison brothers duked it out in turn four.

But he would never forget the day his stalled car cost him a victory over his biggest rival.

His ulcer wouldn't let him. 🏁

By Jeff Owens (2004)

1976 Daytona 500 Top Ten

Finish	Start	No.	Driver	Team/Owner	Laps	Money
1	7	21	David Pearson	Wood Brothers	200	$48,800
2	6	43	Richard Petty	Petty Enterprises	199	35,750
3	32	72	Benny Parsons	L.G. DeWitt	199	23,680
4	11	54	Lennie Pond	Ronnie Elder	198	16,890
5	13	12	Neil Bonnett	Neil Bonnett	197	14,000
6	2	81	Terry Ryan	WAM Racing	186	13,800
7	41	70	J.D. McDuffie	J.D. McDuffie	193	11,260
8	19	63	Terry Bivens	Billy Moyer	193	9,665
9	36	3	Richard Childress	Richard Childress	191	8,990
10	34	79	Frank Warren	Frank Warren	190	8,340

Time of Race: 3 hours, 17 minutes, 8 seconds
Pole Winner: Ramo Stott – 183.456 mph
Average Speed: 152.181 mph
Cautions: 7 for 35 laps
Margin of Victory: 50 yards
Attendance: 125,000

Indiana's Own Makes Motorsports History

Gordon Triumphs In NASCAR's First Crack At Indianapolis

For years, NASCAR had wanted to stage a race at the venerated Indianapolis Motor Speedway. When it finally happened in 1994, even Hollywood could not have imagined the outcome. Jeff Gordon, a Californian by birth, but raised in nearby Pittsboro, Ind., became a part of history when he won NASCAR's inaugural event at Indy. The Hoosier State beamed with pride, and Pittsboro? Suffice it to say it went nuts. Gordon ran well all day, but it came down to a race-closing battle between him and Ernie Irvan. It ended when Irvan suffered a flat tire with four laps to go. And the rest, as they say, is history.

—Steve Waid

Perhaps there could not be a better story. The favorite son of Pittsboro, Ind., the driver they call "The Kid," becomes part of auto racing lore by winning the first NASCAR Winston Cup race ever run at the venerated Indianapolis Motor Speedway.

Twenty-three-year-old Jeff Gordon, the freshest face in NASCAR, enhanced his reputation as a rising superstar by winning the most anticipated Winston Cup race in 35 years – the inaugural Brickyard 400.

To the delight of the fans, who consider him their "hometown" driver, Gordon dominated the race and then, after a furious and thrilling battle with Ernie Irvan during the race's closing laps, emerged victorious by 0.53 second over Brett Bodine.

There could not have been a better scenario for Gordon. A California native raised 15 minutes away from Indianapolis in

Pittsboro, he cut his teeth racing everything from go-karts to Sprints in the Midwest. His career gyrated toward stock cars, and when he snatched up the opportunity to drive in Winston Cup competition with team owner Rick Hendrick in 1993, he thought his chances for driving at Indianapolis were over.

"That's why I kept pushing the rumors about a NASCAR race at Indy when we all started hearing them," Gordon, the 1993 Rookie of the Year, said. "We heard Bill France (NASCAR president) and Tony George (IMS president) were talking about it, and every time I saw Tony, I would say, 'You gotta do it! You gotta do it!'

"And when it happened, well, it was the moment we were all waiting for. Just to be a part of it was very special. But now, to be the winner is more than we could even think of. I'm like a kid in a candy store. I just don't know what to say. It's far beyond words for me."

It's good to be first. Jeff Gordon has no trouble wrapping his arms around this, his most historic win.

Gordon climbs atop the first stock car to grace Indianapolis Motor Speedway's legendary victory lane.

DOZIER MOBLEY PHOTO

Although he has scored wins in the Busch Clash and a 125-Mile Qualifying Race at Daytona, the Brickyard 400 was just the second official Winston Cup win of Gordon's career, and it came in his 50th start. His first victory was the Coca-Cola 600 at Charlotte Motor Speedway on May 29 – which, ironically, was the same day the Indianapolis 500 was run.

At Charlotte, Gordon's emotions spilled over. He cried as he took the checkered flag for his first career win. At Indianapolis, no tears were obvious, but only because a no-less-emotional Gordon held them in check.

"You can't be a crybaby all the time," Gordon said. "But I admit sometimes I can't control my emotions. Winning at Charlotte was a great thrill, and I didn't want my first win to come anywhere else but at Charlotte. But I didn't want my second one to be anywhere but here. And here, we didn't pop a two-tire change to win like we did at Charlotte. We won on the track.

"But I still got emotional. People on the scanners could hear me screaming and yelling over the radio. I had promised myself not to get overemotional. I didn't want to hyperventilate and need oxygen."

Gordon could have been excused if he had hyper-ventilated during the closing laps of the race, when he was locked in a tense duel with Irvan that had the fully packed IMS grandstands yelling with excitement. That scenario had been set up several laps earlier, when Geoff Bodine was forced to retire from the race after a controversial tangle with brother Brett in the fourth turn of the 2.5-mile speedway.

The elder Bodine had been Gordon's only challenger during the early stages of the race, and many anticipated the two would pull away – as they did often – and fight for the victory. Bodine had led 24 laps by the time the field regrouped from the fourth caution period, caused on lap 95 when Mike Chase and Dave Marcis wrecked in the short chute between turns one and two.

After the series of pit stops, Brett Bodine emerged the leader in his King Racing Ford, and Geoff was second in his Ford when the race restarted on lap 100. As they entered the short chute between turns three and four, Geoff went low around his brother to take the lead after tapping him on his rear bumper. But as they sped out on the fourth turn, Brett returned the tap, explaining that it happened because his brother had not sped out of the turn as quickly as he did, and the elder Bodine spun – in front of the entire field.

It could have been a disaster. But cars scattered everywhere, even down pit road, to escape. Only Dale Jarrett, in the Joe Gibbs Racing Chevrolet, crashed with Geoff Bodine. The incident brought out the fifth caution period.

"I don't know what happened to Geoff and Brett," Gordon said. "I didn't see it at all. All I know is he spun, and all I could do was try to keep from hitting him. When I did, well, that's when you know it is your day. Luck is on your side when you are missing wrecks."

With his most persistent challenger on the sidelines, Gordon deduced all he had to do was run a smooth race, avoid mistakes and victory was his to grab. Not so.

Gordon led Brett Bodine when the race restarted on lap 107, with Darrell Waltrip, Rusty Wallace, Ernie Irvan and Bill Elliott in tow. He extended his lead over Bodine, who lost second place to Irvan on lap 115. Irvan was nearly four seconds behind and losing ground.

The leaders completed green-flag pit stops by lap 130 and on the next lap, the sixth and final caution period began after Geoff Brabham and Jimmy Hensley tangled between turns one and two. That brought on another series of pit stops – which were

The entire NASCAR family took to the bricks to commemorate their first trip to racing's most hallowed landmark.

DOZIER MOBLEY PHOTO

the last of the race – and Wallace, in the Penske Racing South Ford, was in front when the green flag flew on lap 135. Gordon was second, followed by Irvan, Bodine, Elliott and Sterling Marlin.

Gordon wasted no time passing Wallace, doing so high in the third turn. As he did so, Irvan moved into second place. Wallace got loose, checked up and lost several positions.

The battle was on. On lap 140, Irvan passed Gordon to take the lead and become the 13th different leader, an Indianapolis record. But he couldn't escape. Gordon hung on his rear bumper and regained the lead on lap 145. Nor could he escape. Irvan snatched the lead back on lap 150.

"The last guy I wanted to race against was Ernie Irvan," said Gordon. "Except maybe Dale Earnhardt.

"It came down to that last pit stop. All of our tires (Goodyears) were excellent, and with each set, we would try and adjust the car. At the end, our car was a little looser than it had been, but that's because each set of tires you get is just a little different.

"I tried to pull away, but no one drives harder than Ernie. When he pulled up on my rear, that would loosen me up. I radioed back to the guys that I had to let him go because I was smoking the tires.

"Then I did the same thing to him. When I got behind him, that would loosen him up, and he had to let me by."

Gordon's plan was to stay behind Irvan until there were only three laps remaining in the 160-lap event. But fate changed his strategy.

On lap 156, Gordon moved to the inside on Irvan in the second turn. After Gordon made the pass, Irvan dropped to the inside of the track and let the pack of cars, led by Bodine, race by. His Ford had suffered a flat right-front tire, and he was removed from the chase, plummeting to a finish of 17th place, one lap down.

"I was waiting until the end, waiting for Ernie to use up his tires," Gordon said. "I drove hard up on him, hoping to get him loose; trying to get as much air off him as I could, and suddenly he went high. I guess it was because his tire went flat. Before that happened, I guarantee you that either we were going into the fence or we were going to cross the finish line side by side."

While Gordon and Irvan raced hard, and often side by side, the pack of Bodine, Elliott, Wallace and Earnhardt gained ground. But when Irvan was removed from contention, Gordon slowly pulled away – and into history.

Bodine's runnerup finish was his best this season with King Racing, which he will be leaving at year's end. Elliott finished third in the Junior Johnson & Associates Ford, Wallace was fourth, Earnhardt fifth in the RCR Enterprises Chevrolet and Waltrip sixth in his Chevrolet. Ken Schrader, Michael Waltrip, Todd Bodine and Morgan Shepherd rounded out the top 10.

With his fifth-place finish and Irvan's demise, Earnhardt retook the lead in the Winston Cup point standings. He is now 27 points ahead of Irvan (2,883-2,856) and came into the race 16 points in arrears.

The six caution periods took up 25 laps. Two drivers, Jimmy Spencer and Chase, were sent to Methodist Hospital for treatment and observation. Spencer sustained a fracture of his right shoulder, the result of a crash on lap 12. It was very doubtful he would drive in the Aug. 14 Bud at the Glen at Watkins Glen, N.Y. Bobby Hillin may drive his Junior Johnson & Associates Ford for him. Chase was to have X-rays taken of his neck, which had sustained contusions and bruises.

Sixteen drivers – an Indy record – finished on the lead lap and 37 of the 43 starters completed the race, tying a NASCAR modern-era record.

Gordon led 93 laps and earned a whopping $613,000, another NASCAR record that eclipsed Kyle Petty's $294,450 for his GM Goodwrench 500 win at Rockingham, N.C., in 1990.

Gordon also went to Disney World, another reward for victory. But as far as he was concerned, he was already in Fantasyland after his day at Indianapolis.

"This is the greatest thing in the world," he said. "It was way past our expectations."

But it happened. And the fans in Indiana could not be happier for "The Kid."

"No," said team owner Rick Hendrick. "It's Mr. Gordon."

By Steve Waid

1994 Brickyard 400 Top Ten

Finish	Start	No.	Driver	Team/Owner	Laps	Money
1	3	24	Jeff Gordon	Hendrick Motorsports	160	$613,000
2	7	26	Brett Bodine	King Racing	160	203,575
3	6	11	Bill Elliott	Junior Johnson &Assoc.	160	164,850
4	12	2	Rusty Wallace	Penske Racing-South	160	140,600
5	2	3	Dale Earnhardt	RCR Enterprises	160	121,625
6	27	17	Darrell Waltrip	DarWal Inc.	160	82,600
7	23	25	Ken Schrader	Hendrick Motorsports	160	77,400
8	15	30	Michael Waltrip	Bahari Racing	160	72,300
9	25	75	Todd Bodine	Butch Mock Motorsports	160	63,600
10	11	21	Morgan Shepherd	Wood Brothers	160	67,350

Time of Race: 3 hours, 1 minutes, 51 seconds
Pole Winner: Rick Mast – 172.414 mph
Average Speed: 131.977 mph
Cautions: 6 for 25 laps
Margin of Victory: 0.53 second
Attendance: 315,000

Petty Makes History With 200th

President Reagan Watches As Petty Wins Firecracker 400

Security at Daytona International Speedway was significantly intensified in anticipation of a special visitor, President Ronald Reagan. Reagan was in the radio booth and witnessed an exciting duel between Richard Petty and Cale Yarborough. They were side by side as they sped to a race-ending caution flag. Petty nipped Yarborough to earn his historic 200th career victory. Ironically, few people remember that Yarborough pulled onto pit road before taking the checkered flag, allowing Harry Gant to finish second. After the race, Petty met the president in the press box and later joined him and other drivers for a special post-race luncheon in the garage area. The victory would be Petty's last.

—Steve Waid

Independence Day 1984 has become the most significant date in stock car racing history.

Richard Lee Petty of Level Cross, N.C., the long-reigning "King of Stock Car Racing," made history by winning his 200th NASCAR Winston Cup race.

More than that, he did it before an astonished president of the United States and 80,000 excited, cheering fans who watched him bang metal with Cale Yarborough in a furious battle down the homestretch in today's Pepsi Firecracker 400 at Daytona International Speedway.

The drama came to a heart-stopping end when Petty nudged his STP Pontiac across the finish line a fender-length ahead of Yarborough's overwhelmingly favored Ranier/Hardee's Chevrolet Monte Carlo.

No one could have conceived a better setting. The legendary Petty won his 200th race – more than any other NASCAR driver in history – on America's 208th birthday in front of Ronald Reagan, the first president to attend a Winston Cup event. The gut-wrenching finish will be logged in Daytona records as one of the most memorable.

Even Petty, who turned 47 on July 2, recognized the impact of the race. Routinely at ease in victory and defeat during the course of this 25-year career, he was obviously touched, swallowing hard and visibly struggling for the right words to say. At times he even appeared to be fighting to hold back tears.

"I just want to say how much of a pleasure it's been working with you guys," Petty said to the media gathered in the speedway press box. "Not that I'm quitting or anything. It's just a situation where Richard Petty won 200 races, but he couldn't do it by himself. I guess first I should thank STP, which has been with me for 14 years. There were a couple years when I didn't win and a lot of people had written me off, but STP stuck with me.

"All of the people who have worked with me have been super. I can't tell you how I feel about the people who have been involved in this situation. I've got a gift in this talent that God gave me and there have been a lot of people who have helped me over the years.

Richard Petty led six times for 53 laps en route to his 200th career win.

"I appreciate all of them. Two hundred wins at a local track would be nothing, but that's where the press comes in. You got the word out to people.

"I felt the same way I did after any win, but it's a big thrill to hear the crew hollering over the radio and the crowd cheering. The 200th victory was a big win. Because it was Daytona, it was a big win. It was a big deal because it was July 4th. And it was the first race for a president. All of that combined to make it just a big, big deal. That's the best way to describe it."

Although the race covered 160 laps on Daytona's 2.5-mile trioval, Petty actually won it on the 158th lap. He had been leading the relentless Yarborough, who was obviously poised to make the classic last-lap "slingshot" pass for victory, when Doug Heveron lost control of his car at the entrance to the first turn and flipped into the infield.

Fortunately the rookie, Heveron, was not injured in the incident, but everyone knew what the resulting caution flag – only the third of the day – meant.

Petty and Yarborough took the yellow flag after they crossed the start-finish line to begin lap 158, which meant they had to race each other back to the flag stand. It was clear that the winner of the dash would be the winner of the race.

Petty led down the backstretch, but going into the 31-degree third turn, Yarborough slipped by and assumed first place. However, in so doing, he charged into the turn too hard, and his Monte Carlo drifted high into the turn. Petty cut to the inside immediately, and the two raced side by side as they gobbled up the last half-mile of the race at 200 miles per hour.

Touching metal as they bore down on the slower cars, Petty got the edge with his inside route. He picked up the draft of the cars ahead, and his last contact with Yarborough squirted him ahead by a mere couple feet. That turned out

to be the margin of victory.

Petty's STP crew erupted in a dance of celebration because they knew, as did all in attendance, all Petty had to do was follow the pace car to the checkered flag.

"Where did I want to be on that lap?" Petty said during the winner's interview. "Exactly where I am now. As Cale followed me before we got the caution, I didn't have the foggiest idea of what I was going to do. It was a circumstance where someone would act, and I would react. I knew what Cale would do, and I knew what I wanted to do if he did it.

"But then came the caution. When we came off the fourth turn, we couldn't see what happened in the first turn. But when we crossed the line, we saw the turn and, the first thing you do is look. The minute I saw that car in the infield I knew what had to be done. I didn't even look for a caution, although I think I saw the yellow light in the first turn. I just knew that the first car to the finish line would be the winner."

Petty admitted he got a break when Yarborough got a bit too high in the third turn. "Cale was trying so hard that he ran in there harder than he would have liked, I'm sure," said Petty. "When he burped the car to keep it from going into the wall, I just turned left, and I was under him. I had some advantage because I was able to use the draft of three or four slower cars ahead of us (among them Ken Ragan's and David Pearson's). At first, I thought they would be a detriment because they would block me."

Using the traffic, Petty squeezed closer to Yarborough, who was still hung on the outside. It appeared their cars had been welded together.

"We touched two or three times there, but not enough to upset either car," allowed Petty. "I think the last time we touched, it squirted me in front of Cale, maybe two or three feet. All I know is from

where I was sitting I was in front of him. We never touched hard enough to lose the line. We kept it up from where the entrance to pit road starts to maybe 50 feet in front of the finish line."

All that remained after the duel was for Petty and Yarborough to cruise the final two laps at reduced speed. But the finishing order changed when the normally alert Yarborough brought his car down pit road as Petty took the white flag. Thinking the race was over, Yarborough had begun to make his way into the garage area when he suddenly realized there was one lap remaining. He roared down pit road and back on the track, but not before he had lost second place to Harry Gant in the Skoal Bandit Monte Carlo.

"My brain blew up, I guess," said Yarborough, the pole winner who came so close to winning his fourth race in only nine starts this season. "I just flat messed up. I misread the flagman's fingers, and I thought the race was over. I was thinking so much about beating Richard to the flag that for some reason I thought the race was over.

"I guess a late caution flag is something you can't anticipate. It came out as we went into turn one, and I knew I had to beat him to the flag. I got around him going into turn three, but I went into it harder than I wanted to, and that let him get under me. There were some slower cars ahead, and he got to use their draft while I got hung on the outside.

"I was sitting right where I wanted to be, but Richard was awfully strong, and he edged me to the line. He ran a heckuva race, and I congratulate him on his 200th win. Now he can get started on 300."

Petty's win was the 10th of his career at Daytona, a track that has been good to him (witness his record seven Daytona 500 triumphs). His last Pepsi Firecracker 400 win came in 1977.

His 200th win came in his 944th start (also a record), and he has now logged 536 top-five finishes

and 644 among the top 10. His winnings of $43,755 boosted his season total to $156,125 and his career winnings to $5,610,657, another record.

Yarborough showed his muscle by leading nine times for 79 laps, but Petty was his anticipated strong self as he led six times for 53 laps.

"Really, I can't say that I had the strongest car," said Petty. "After our last pit stops (on laps 123 and 124), I made up some seconds on Cale. But he ran me down."

Petty had about a six-second lead following the stops, but by lap 142, Yarborough had caught them. "His car was probably a little quicker," admitted Petty. "But they were fairly equal."

Gant's runnerup finish was the 17th of his career and his 11th on a superspeedway. Thus maintaining his long-established bridesmaid role.

Following Yarborough in fourth place was Bobby Allison in the DiGard/Miller High Life Buick. Fifth place went to Benny Parsons in the Hayes/Copenhagen Monte Carlo, sixth to Bill Elliott in the Coors/Melling Ford Thunderbird, seventh to Terry Labonte in the Hagan/Piedmont Airlines Monte Carlo, eighth to Dale Earnhardt in the Childress/Wrangler Monte Carlo, ninth to Neil Bonnett in the Johnson-Hodgdon/Budweiser Monte Carlo and 10th to Joe Ruttman in the

Benfield/Levi Garrett Monte Carlo.

Ignition problems forced Darrell Waltrip's Johnson-Hodgdon/Budweiser Monte Carlo into an early 31-lap pit stop. Upon returning to the race, he could complete only 126 laps. He finished 31st.

Buddy Baker also experienced a blown engine in his Wood Brothers/Valvoline Thunderbird, and he completed only four laps en route to a 41st-place finish. That was only slightly better than Lake Speed, who was unable to complete the first lap before the engine in his Ellington/Bull Frog Knits Monte Carlo let go, relegating him to a 42nd-place finish.

Bobby Hillin's wreck in the second turn brought out the day's second caution on lap 143 (Baker's blown engine brought out the first), while Heveron's accident initiated the third and final caution of the day. The three yellow flags totaled 15 laps. That permitted Petty to win with an average speed of 171.204 mph.

Eight drivers swapped the lead 29 times, and the race took two hours, 19 minutes and 59 seconds to complete.

That was also the amount of time it took to create racing history.

"I would say that going for the 200th win was more of a burden rather than a pressure situation for me," said Petty, who spent the past several weeks besieged with questions about the quest.

"No one even mentioned it until I got win number 199 (in the May Budweiser 500 at Dover, Del.). I guess it would have gone on for a year if it had taken me that long to get it. I'm just glad I could get in within five races."

Now that the hunt is done and the goal achieved, Richard Petty can savor the memory and proceed with the business at hand – winning races. On July 4, 1984, he proved conclusively he's more than able to do that. 🏁

By Steve Waid

1984 Firecracker 400 Top Ten

Finish	Start	No.	Driver	Team/Owner	Laps	Money
1	6	43	Richard Petty	Curb Motorsports	160	$43,755
2	13	33	Harry Gant	Mach 1 Racing	160	25,570
3	1	28	Cale Yarborough	Ranier-Lundy	160	23,640
4	19	22	Bobby Allison	DiGard	160	21,850
5	9	55	Benny Parsons	Johnny Hayes	160	10,450
6	3	9	Bill Elliott	Melling Racing	160	14,050
7	4	44	Terry Labonte	Billy Hagan	159	11,975
8	2	3	Dale Earnhardt	RCR Enterprises	159	13,600
9	20	12	Neil Bonnett	Johnson-Hodgdon	159	7,655
10	18	98	Joe Ruttman	Ron Benfield	157	9,255

Time of Race: 2 hours, 19 minutes, 59 seconds
Pole Winner: Cale Yarborough – 199.743 mph
Average Speed: 171.204 mph
Cautions: 3 for 15 laps
Margin of Victory: Under Caution
Attendance: 80,000

1987 The Winston

It's Earnhardt In The Wild Winston

Earnhardt Wins Amid Controversial Finish

After NASCAR's "all star" race was created in 1985, it went through several changes in an effort to create more excitement. By 1987, a 10-lap, race-closing "shootout" had been created. Bill Elliott was the race's dominant driver, but when the final 10 laps began, he and Dale Earnhardt began banging on each other. As they raced down the dogleg on the frontstretch, Elliott whacked Earnhardt into the grass. Remarkably, Earnhardt kept control and never gave up the lead. He went on to win amid a great deal of controversy. The race is famous for Earnhardt's "pass in the grass" that actually wasn't. "I got knocked into the grass!" Earnhardt said repeatedly over the years afterward.

—Steve Waid

They wanted a shootout in the third annual running of The Winston. They got it. And an argument or two. And some blown tempers. And a fistfight. And a lot more.

In a wham, bam, controversial 10-lap dash finish, Dale Earnhardt spectacularly avoided disaster and withstood the rage of his rivals to record the victory worth $200,000 at the 1.5 mile Charlotte Motor Speedway. In doing so, Earnhardt became the third different winner in the three-year history of the event and spoiled what had been the perfect dominance of Bill Elliott, who humbled the field in the first two segments of the special race by leading 121 of the 125 laps therein.

So, it came as no surprise that Elliott was frustrated after his loss but, beyond that, he was furious with what he felt were Earnhardt's unsportsmanlike, and dangerous, tactics en route to the victory.

The scenario:

The first segment of the event, which ran 75 laps, ended with just three men, Elliott in the Coors/Melling Ford Thunderbird, Geoff Bodine in the Hendrick/Levi Garrett Chevrolet Monte Carlo SS, and Kyle Petty in the Wood Brothers/Citgo Ford, sharing the lead. Elliott led 71 of those 75 laps.

Segment Two: It began after a 10-minute delay during which all 20 teams in the event made NASCAR-legal alterations to their cars. Nearly all did while Elliott took on four tires and patiently awaited the green flag. No other work was done to his car.

The race resumed and, again, Elliott dominated, if that is a strong enough word. He led all 50 laps of the segment and, when it ended, Earnhardt was running second.

Then came the ten-lap trophy dash. Under the new format of The Winston, these ten laps must be run under green. Cautions do not count. It's what everyone had been waiting for.

Elliott started on the pole, with Bodine second and Petty third – they are the only race leaders, hence they received the top three starting spots. Earnhardt is in fourth. On the start of the first lap, Bodine jumped to a quick start and nudged ahead

After a wild day on and off the tracks, Earnhardt became the third different winner in the three-year history of The Winston.

DAVID CHOBAT PHOTO

Despite almost coming to post-race blows with Bill Elliott's crew, Team Childress is all smiles in victory lane.

DAVID CHOBAT PHOTO

of Elliott. But, going into the second turn, Bodine's Chevrolet turned sideways after contact with Elliott's Ford. Bodine looped his car and, remarkably, no one made contact.

But, as that happened, Earnhardt, who had moved into third, shot to the inside and found himself all alone in the lead. The complexion of the race changed dramatically. Even so, it marks the first episode that Elliott will later recall as another disreputable Earnhardt driving tactic.

The caution was displayed and Bodine made a pit stop to change tires. Elliott recovered from the mishap suitably enough to run second to Earnhardt and give chase. There's no doubt he has enough strength in his car, but Earnhardt's team has made enough adjustments to his during the two ten-minute stops to ensure that it, too, is stout.

Elliott immediately rode Earnhardt's rear bumper. Just seven laps from the finish, it becomes clear the war is for real. Coming out of the fourth turn, their cars make contact and Earnhardt is sent into the infield grass at the front trioval. In a remarkable display of driving talent, Earnhardt keeps the car on a straight line through a 150-foot plowing job and roars back onto the asphalt, holding his advantage. But, as he later explained, his hackles were up.

One lap later. As the duo raced into the third turn, Elliott came to the outside of Earnhardt. Clearly displeased with what transpired earlier, Earnhardt squeezed Elliott to the wall. He claimed he never made contact. Elliott said otherwise and allowed that it was at this point Earnhardt's maneuver crumpled the left-rear fender onto the tire. The damage was sufficient to cut the tire, resulting in its demise just a lap later.

While the two drivers indulged in this episode, Terry Labonte snaked into the lead in his Johnson/Budweiser Chevrolet. But his advantage did not last long. Earnhardt roared past by the time the

field raced into the first turn. He went on to win by 0.74 second. Elliott, after a pit stop to change tires, came home 14th.

But that was far from the end of it. On the final lap, Elliott's Ford limped around the track like a crippled soldier. As Earnhardt raced toward the checkered flag, an obvious winner over Labonte, he closed in on the Coors/Melling Ford. Suddenly, on the backstretch, Elliott's car found life and sped toward the finish line.

Then, on the "cool-down" lap, Elliott's displeasure became obvious. He blocked Earnhardt coming out of the first turn. On the backstretch, he turned toward Earnhardt, on the outside, and forced him to hit the brakes so hard smoke billowed from the tires. He cut his rival off at the entrance to pit road and then, at the entrance to the garage area, he once again turned toward Earnhardt and forced him to move to the outside of pit road.

This was done in the presence of the Wrangler crew, who, ironically, pitted just one space away from Elliott's team. Words were exchanged; fists shook.

It wasn't over. In the garage area, Kyle Petty and Rusty Wallace, driver of the Blue Max/Kodiak Grand Prix 2+2, exchanged blows and were separated by Richard Petty, Kyle's father.

The final rundown showed that behind Earnhardt and Labonte, Tim Richmond finished third in his first race in the Hendrick/Folgers Chevrolet since being felled by double pneumonia in December. Bodine wound up fourth, with Wallace fifth, Kyle Petty sixth, Morgan Shepherd seventh in the Bernstein/Quaker State Buick LaSabre, Bobby Allison eighth in the Stavola/Miller American Buick, Darrell Waltrip ninth in the Hendrick/Tide Chevrolet and Benny Parsons tenth in the Jackson/Copenhagen Oldsmobile Delta 88.

Elliott earned $110,150 for his day's work, $100,000 of which came in leader bonuses through

the race's first two segments. He stood to pocket $300,000 with a victory.

His side of the tale:

"It really got started (on the final 10 laps) at the start. The pace car didn't get out of the way quickly enough. Geoff got a good start but the pace car was in my way and I couldn't keep up. When we got to the corner, Earnhardt got in front of me and he turned left on me. He hit me. I don't know what happened with Bodine, whether he cut down on me or what, but the next thing I know we are both spinning all of a sudden.

"A lot of things are going on when the green flag drops. I don't know exactly what happened, but it was a situation that never should have happened.

"Then we went into the fourth turn and Earnhardt turned left on me and tried to run me through the grass. I did what I could to keep us both off the grass and wrecking. Then the next thing, well, when a man pulls alongside you and tries to run you into the wall, that's pretty obvious. I had the position. He let me get alongside him and then turned into me. That's when the tire was cut. It crumpled the left fender onto the tire and a couple of laps later it blew. You look at the tape. He hit me several times. The fans saw it. You saw it.

"Yes, when the race was over, I was still ticked off. I admit it. If a man has to run over you to beat you,

Earnhardt and Childress enjoy another trip to victory lane.
DAVID CHOBAT PHOTO

it's time to stop. I'm sick of it. Everyone knows his style. I am sick and tired of it. If that is what it takes to be the Winston Cup champion, I don't want it.

"The aggressiveness has gotten out of hand. This is not Saturday night wrestling. I've been to Talladega, Daytona and everywhere else and I'm beat up by the same guy.

"Yes, I'm frustrated. My car worked good here. It ran good. I think that was obvious. If you had a car that ran that good only to have it all taken away from you the way it was, how would you feel?

"I think that more than racing, he discredits his sponsor and himself. But I have nothing to say to him. If that is the way he wants to win races, then I hope he wins 1,000 of them. He'll be doing it all on Saturday nights."

With his victory, Earnhardt laid claim to wins in the last four Charlotte events. He swept both the Coca-Cola and the Oakwood Homes 500 in Winston Cup competition last year and won the fall All-Pro 300 Busch Series race. For his career, he has won $709,748 in Winston Cup competition at CMS and $885,673 overall. In the last 12 months, the total is $380,200 for Winston Cup racing, $455,095 overall.

His comments after The Winston:

"Bodine and Elliott wrecked in the first turn. I guess Bodine chopped down on him and turned him around, but all I know is that I didn't touch anybody. I guess it was reflexes. I checked up and I started to move where I thought they wouldn't be. I decided to go to the bottom of the track and I was by myself. I don't know why they threw the caution flag. No one was stopped.

"Then, as we came into the trioval two laps later, Elliott got under me and clipped me sideways. I almost got the car started the other way before I went into the grass and then I was able to get it right while I was in it. If I hadn't, I might have gone right

up into the flagstand right there with Harold Kinder (flagman). I can guarantee you that, if I had turned someone side-ways like that, I would be hanging from the flagpole right now.

"I wasn't upset earlier, but that got me upset.

"On the next lap, he got alongside me on the outside and I took him up the track, but I never touched him. That's when Labonte got by and I knew then I had to race him.

"Bill got frustrated. Look, if I had done what he had through the first two segments of the race only to lose in the last 10 laps, I would be frustrated, too. He waited on me after the checkered flag and then tried to run me into the wall. That was very unsportsmanlike. After that, I tried to stay away from him. I motioned my crew to stay away from his. This was between me and Bill. Not between Ernie (Elliott's brother and crew chief) or anyone else. No one else was on the track.

"I'm not mad at Elliott. I know he was frustrated. If he wants to carry this on, then we will. I will stand flatfooted against him."

Said Cecil Gordon, the former driver who serves as the shop foreman for the Wrangler team owned by Richard Childress: "All you have to do is print what you saw. We've taken the heat from NASCAR at Bristol (Tenn.) and Richmond (Va.) and to have what happened after the race was over, well NASCAR has to do something about it."

Elliott agreed, but in a different way: "I think the only way to stop this is to start fining points. Take them away in cases like this."

NASCAR officials,

who stated in the pre-race drivers' meeting that no protests would be allowed since The Winston was a special event that awarded no points, said that they would study videotapes of the final 10 laps and, if needed, make a determination of disciplinary action within a few days.

Elliott won the pole for the event with a track record of 170.827 mph, posted in time trials on May 16. That bettered the one-lap mark of 169.252 mph set by Richmond last October. Richmond was second in qualifying with a lap of 170.23 mph in the Hendrick/Folgers Chevrolet, while Davey Allison was the third man to beat the record with a lap of 169.274 mph in the Ranier/Havoline Ford.

For the record, Earnhardt now has won seven of the 10 events staged this season, although The Winston has no part in the Winston Cup championship and is not listed as an official event as such. He won with an average speed of 153.023 mph. The race had only one official caution flag, thrown when Neil Bonnett and Richard Petty collided in the fourth turn on lap 64. Bonnett, taken to Cabarrus Memorial Hospital for treatment, was released with water on his elbow and right knee. His arm was placed in a sling.

By Steve Waid

1987 The Winston Top Ten

Finish	Start	No.	Driver	Team/Owner	Laps	Money
1	4	3	Dale Earnhardt	RCR Enterprises	135	$200,000
2	12	11	Terry Labonte	Junior Johnson	135	50,000
3	2	25	Tim Richmond	Hendrick Motorsports	135	40,000
4	5	5	Geoff Bodine	Hendrick Motorsports	135	30,000
5	7	27	Rusty Wallace	Blue Max Racing	135	19,000
6	15	21	Kyle Petty	Wood Brothers	135	14,000
7	17	26	Morgan Shepherd	King Motorsports	135	12,000
8	14	22	Bobby Allison	Stavola Brothers	135	11,400
9	9	17	Darrell Waltrip	Hendrick Motorsports	135	11,250
10	6	55	Benny Parsons	Jackson Brothers	135	10,900

Time of Race: 1 hour, 19 minutes, 24 seconds (run in three segments)
Pole Winner: Bill Elliott – based on points – no time trials
Average Speed: 153.023 mph
Cautions: 1 (laps did not count)
Margin of Victory: 0.74 second
Attendance: 59,500

Earnhardt leads the field, something he did often on his way to victory lane.

DOZIER MOBLEY PHOTO

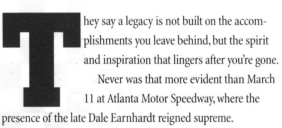

10

Emotional Rescue

Harvick's Feel-Good Win Boosts Spirits Of RCR, Rest Of Cup Community

The NASCAR world was still engulfed in sadness following the death of Dale Earnhardt in the Daytona 500. A virtual unknown named Kevin Harvick had been picked to replace Earnhardt. The car he drove was still adorned with its familiar black and silver colors, but the number had been changed from 3 to 29. No one expected much out of Harvick. But at Atlanta Motor Speedway, he took the lead with five laps to go and then held off a charging Jeff Gordon to take the victory in only his third start. It was a stunning and highly emotional victory that left many in tears.

—Steve Waid

They say a legacy is not built on the accomplishments you leave behind, but the spirit and inspiration that lingers after you're gone.

Never was that more evident than March 11 at Atlanta Motor Speedway, where the presence of the late Dale Earnhardt reigned supreme.

It was his inspiration that sparked the team he left behind to victory just three weeks after his tragic death.

It was his hard-charging attitude that propelled young Kevin Harvick, his rookie replacement, to one of the most improbable victories in Winston Cup history.

And it was his legacy – one paid tribute to throughout another race weekend – that left a surreal feeling hanging over the Georgia track hours after one of the most thrilling finishes and one of the most emotional days NASCAR has ever experienced.

"I don't know quite how to explain what just happened," said runnerup Jeff Gordon, who lost by inches to the car that Earnhardt drove to a record seven Winston Cup championships.

"God blesses us all in a lot of ways," Gordon said. "He's defi-

nitely watching over that team right now. I think there was a higher power who wanted to see that outcome."

To many, the higher power was Earnhardt, whose shocking death on the final lap of the Feb. 18 Daytona 500 rocked the NASCAR world.

With his team and most of the NASCAR community still reeling over his death, what the sport and his team needed more than anything was a dramatic, spine-tingling finish, the type that made Earnhardt a legend.

They got it in true Earnhardt fashion. Harvick, a baby-faced, 25-year-old driver making just his third Winston Cup start, made a daring three-wide pass in turn four to take the lead with just five laps to go. He then held off Gordon, a three-time champion with 53 career victories, in a photo finish eerily similar to Earnhardt's win over Bobby Labonte in the same race a year ago.

His victory set off a celebration that struck an emotional chord with nearly everyone in attendance and millions watching at home.

As Harvick's crew leaped over the pit wall, the grandstands

Harvick drove with a heavy heart and under the weight of extraordinary expectations, but had no trouble hoisting the heavy trophy.

NS ARCHIVE PHOTO

erupted into a thunder of cheers that drowned out the roar of the cars trying to complete the race. Car owner Richard Childress, who owned Earnhardt's famous black No. 3, and his teammates wept for joy, a show of jubilation they wondered if they would ever experience again after their hero's death.

Harvick, meanwhile, spun his white Chevrolet around in a cloud of tire smoke on the frontstretch, leaving black marks on the pavement similar to the ones that marked Earnhardt's historic victory in the 1998 Daytona 500.

He then circled the track holding three fingers in the air, the same salute Earnhardt's fans had delivered on lap 3 of the race. As he headed to victory lane, crew after crew lined up on pit road to congratulate him, another moment last seen when Earnhardt finally won the Daytona 500 after 20 tries.

As Harvick pulled into victory lane, rivals Dale Jarrett and Gordon sprinted down pit road to congratulate Earnhardt's old team. Throughout the garage, drivers and crewmen were in awe of what they had just witnessed, an inspiring victory by a team that had sunk to the depths of depression three weeks before.

"We all care a lot about each other," Gordon said. "This is an extended family and that team has been through a lot. To go through what they went through and rebound today, it was just a happy moment for a lot of people."

Even a dejected Dale Earnhardt Jr., who lost his own chance at victory when he cut a tire during the mad scramble for the lead during the final laps, couldn't help but congratulate his father's team.

"The competitor in me is a little jealous," said Junior, who had hopes of honoring his father in victory lane. "But I'm real happy for Richard and the team. It really makes me feel good to go home knowing those guys have something to celebrate."

Throughout the NASCAR world, Earnhardt's memory and career were finally celebrated the only place they truly could be – in victory lane.

"I'm speechless," Darrell Waltrip, one of Earnhardt's oldest rivals, told the Fox Sports audience. "You can't imagine what this means to these people. This is an incredible moment in our sport."

It was a moment the whole sport needed after three gut-wrenching weeks following Earnhardt's death.

"This will make it a lot better for everybody to try to heal a little quicker," said Kevin Hamlin, Earnhardt and Harvick's crew chief. "We still have one thing in mind. We're racing hard for one really big reason right now, and that's to do the very best we can in Dale's memory."

Earnhardt would have been ecstatic about what he saw at Atlanta, a track he had put his stamp on with a record nine victories.

"He's up there smiling right now, knowing that we did what he wanted," an emotional Childress said.

Two weeks ago, many in the national media were appalled that NASCAR returned to action just one week after the on-track death of its biggest star. They were even more stunned that Earnhardt's team came back with a freshly painted car and a new driver.

But it was all according to the plan – Earnhardt's plan.

After former driver Neil Bonnett, one of his closest friends, was killed in a 1994 crash at Daytona, Earnhardt made Childress promise their team would carry on if the same thing happened to him.

"He said, 'If something like that happens to me, you go race this race team and keep going,'" Childress said.

A few years later, they had a similar conversation after Childress tumbled down a mountain while hunting in New Mexico. Beaten and battered, Childress made Earnhardt promise that he, too, would carry on without him.

"I told him if I hadn't made it out of that, you had better race the next week," Childress said. "We both knew what we wanted to do."

What they wanted was to race and to win, just as they had done 67 times in the past 17 years. And

Crew members from every team line up to congratulate Harvick on his achievement.

The entire RCR family found reason to smile on this day.

NS ARCHIVE PHOTO

they both knew who they wanted to carry on the Earnhardt legacy.

Earnhardt had watched Harvick race Childress' Busch Series car last year and was so impressed he tried to hire him for his own Dale Earnhardt Inc. team. To Childress, Earnhardt's replacement was a given. He knew Harvick would have Earnhardt's blessing.

"What he wanted was to get an aggressive driver who could go out and win," Childress said. "He wanted somebody in the race car who could keep this team together."

In just his third Winston Cup race, and his first 500-miler, Harvick lived up to Earnhardt's expectations, scoring his first career victory quicker than anyone in Winston Cup's modern era. His perseverance and aggressive style made believers out of many.

During the final, dramatic showdown, Harvick put himself in position for an Earnhardt-like charge to the front. After chasing leaders Jarrett, Gordon and Jerry Nadeau most of the day, he made a daring three-wide pass by Jarrett and Nadeau with just five laps remaining.

After all three crossed the start/finish line side-by-side, Harvick pulled ahead in turn one and darted away. When Gordon ran him down on the final lap, he held his line like a veteran, taking the checkered flag 6/1,000ths of a second ahead of Gordon.

The remarkable pass for the lead and photo finish were reminiscent of the man he replaced.

"He made the move that won the race," Gordon said. "He didn't have the best car, but he made the move. It's hard to say that's a rookie move. It looked like a veteran to me."

"We rode around for 450 miles and it was finally time to give it everything you had," Harvick said. "That's never been my nature, to give up. That's the biggest thing I learned at RCR, even when you're having a bad day, you get all you can get, and today, it happened to be for the win."

"That's the same way Kevin and this whole team is," Childress said. "We've got that no-give-up attitude. That's the way Dale was."

Aside from his family, no one has been hit harder by Earnhardt's death than Childress, one of his closest friends and his partner for nearly 20 years.

As NASCAR continues to investigate Earnhardt's crash and consider safety measures that might prevent similar fatalities, and as fans and race tracks pay weekly tributes to the former champion, Childress is constantly reminded of the man with whom he spent much of his life and career.

"I used to think I wasn't very emotional," he says. "I guess I've found out lately how soft I really am."

Harvick's performance, coupled with a new wave of Earnhardt memories, stirred up emotions that had him choking back tears during most of the post-race celebrations.

"It brings back memories ... all day long has," he said. "This is a very emotional time for me and my race team. We've done a lot of praying together. These are the most adverse situations I think a race team or any kind of team could be put in. ... But not having to worry about the race team has been a big relief. Kevin stepped in and took away a lot of the pain."

And replaced it with joy the likes of which Childress thought he'd never experience again. But thanks to Harvick – and Earnhardt – he did.

"The last five or six laps when we got the lead, I just looked up in the sky and said, 'I need your help old buddy,' and he was there," Childress said.

"I know he is up there looking down. I could see his mustache break out with that big old smile."

By Jeff Owens

2001 Cracker Barrel 500 Top Ten

Finish	Start	No.	Driver	Team/Owner	Laps	Money
1	5	29	Kevin Harvick	RCR	325	$158,427
2	2	24	Jeff Gordon	Hendrick Motorsports	325	143,077
3	13	25	Jerry Nadeau	Hendrick Motorsports	325	80,650
4	1	88	Dale Jarrett	Robert Yates Racing	325	114,927
5	21	5	Terry Labonte	Hendrick Motorsports	325	92,630
6	23	28	Ricky Rudd	Robert Yates Racing	325	77,367
7	19	10	Johnny Benson	MBV Motorsports	325	52,295
8	27	36	Ken Schrader	MB2 Motorsports	324	61,005
9	30	31	Mike Skinner	RCR	324	75,194
10	36	97	Kurt Busch	Roush Racing	324	56,945

Time of Race: 3 hours, 29 minutes, 36 seconds
Pole Winner: Dale Jarrett – 192.748 mph
Average Speed: 143.273 mph
Cautions: 8 for 42 laps
Margin of Victory: 0.006 second
Attendance: 124,000

11

Wow! Elliott Is One In A Million

Elliott Wins And History Is Made

Amid a crush of publicity, Bill Elliott arrived at Darlington Raceway as the driver who could earn the first "Winston Million" bonus for winning three of four selected races. The money was his if he won the Southern 500. For a while, it seemed the money was safe. Harry Gant, Dale Earnhardt and Cale Yarborough all appeared to have the race won at one time or another. But misfortune struck them all, and Elliott took the win and earned the $1 million bonus at a time when no other race car driver in history had won $1 million in a single season.

—Steve Waid

He did it.

Bill Elliott won the Southern 500 NASCAR Winston Cup race and a $1 million bonus in such a way that it could only have been destined; written in tablets of stone.

Only after his team corrected an ill-handling car and he later dodged a couple of excruciatingly close, nearly disastrous incidents was Elliott able to make racing history. As nerve-racking as it all had to be, he was seemingly guided by the hand of Divine Providence.

Elliott's Southern 500 victory earned him $1 million from R.J. Reynolds Tobacco Co. in its Winston Million program. It meant that the driver from Dawsonville, Ga., had reached a whopping $1,857,243 in season winnings and thus set the all-time auto racing record, doubling the old mark held by Mario Andretti. Assuming that Elliott wins the 1985 Winston Cup championship – and all the cash awards therein – it will mean

that he can top $2.4 million in season winnings.

Elliott was in the position to win the $1 million because he had already won two of the four selected events in the Winston Million program – the Daytona 500 and the Winston 500. A victory in the Southern 500 at Darlington International Raceway gave him the money because he was the first driver to win three of the four events that compose the program. The World 600 at Charlotte, N.C., was the other event.

Further, Elliott won his 10th superspeedway race of his spectacular 1985 season. That tied him with David Pearson as the only other competitor to win that many big-track races in a single year. With five superspeedway events left in '85, Elliott stands an excellent chance at setting the all-time record.

But obviously the win did not come easily. It was a typical, bizarre Southern 500, littered by a modern-day record 14 caution flags for 70 laps and fateful mechanical problems for some of the day's top competitors.

Hot off the press! Elliott and former RJR CEO Jerry Long preview this $1M headline.

DAVID CHOBAT PHOTO

Winning the million was a team effort. Elliott's crew worked with quick precision in the South Carolina sun.

DAVID CHOBAT PHOTO

"Thanks to the good Lord for looking out for me today," said Elliott. "A lot of things happened, and that wasn't unexpected. But I was able to keep my cool and keep the car together. That way I could race the track all day and let the others race themselves. And what a day it was. It was the toughest race I've ever run."

It started well enough for Elliott, who won the pole position and led the first 14 laps. But it was quickly evident that his Coors/Melling Ford Thunderbird was not the model of perfection it had been for most of the season.

Dale Earnhardt soon took command, and the driver of the Childress/Wrangler Chevrolet Monte Carlo was to ultimately lead five times for 147 laps.

Moving to the forefront with him was Harry Gant, the race's defending champion who drove the Skoal Bandit Monte Carlo to the lead four times for 84 laps.

As Earnhardt and Gant swapped the lead, Elliott drifted back as far as fourth place. He was losing ground because his chassis setup – far from what he would have wanted – was causing excessive tire wear.

"We were really down on our luck halfway through the race," said Elliott, who realized that Gant and Earnhardt were putting him nearly a half-second behind with each succeeding lap. "The car wasn't the way I had hoped it would be."

After a series of green-flag stops on laps 259-263, Gant retained his lead, and Elliott was a distant 19.26 seconds behind in fourth place. Earnhardt was second and Cale Yarborough, in the Ranier/Hardee's Thunderbird, was third.

Elliott, in fact, was dangerously close to blowing a severely-blistered left rear tire when fate stepped in for the first time. On lap 267, Clark Dwyer spun his Sunny King Thunderbird and brought out the day's eighth caution. This allowed Elliott's crew to change

tires and make a much-needed chassis adjustment. When the race restarted on lap 273, Elliott was still in fourth place, but he was only three seconds behind Gant and running much smoother.

The ninth caution of the day on lap 294 afforded the Coors/Melling crew another chance to adjust the chassis, and then, when the race restarted on lap 299, fate was again kind to Elliott.

Gant suddenly and inexplicably suffered a dropped valve and fell out of the chase. He limped around on seven cylinders for several laps but ultimately retired his Monte Carlo with a blown engine after completing 336 laps.

Then, on lap 318, good fortune smiled on Elliott again. Earnhardt, who had masterfully manhandled his car all day as he overcame persistent tire stagger problems – flirting with danger all the while – spun in the second turn of the 1.366-mile Darlington track. He was in second place behind Yarborough but directly in front of Elliott.

There are some who may never know how

Elliott missed Earnhardt. As Earnhardt came off the second-turn wall and looped toward the apron, Elliott shot by low, missing the Wrangler Monte Carlo by inches. It was a very tense moment.

"I don't know how I got by," said Elliott, "I saw Dale go up against the wall, so I went low. Then he came down, and I just closed my eyes."

Elliott took the lead for the first time since the 100th lap on laps 319-322, which were run under the caution, but lost the lead on lap 323 when Yarborough shot by to retake command.

Yarborough's lead was to last just one lap. As it sped into the fourth turn, smoke poured from Yarborough's Thunderbird, and it was assumed he had suffered a blown engine. However, the problem was a broken steering line, which dumped fluid and created the smoke.

As it was with Earnhardt, Elliott was right behind Yarborough at the time of the incident, and again, he was fortunate.

"I thought at first Cale had blown an engine,"

said Elliott. "There was a bit of fluid on the track, but I was able to get through it, get down to the apron and get around Cale. It was touchy at first, but there wasn't a problem after that."

Yarborough's problem created the day's 11th caution period, and when it ended on lap 329, Elliott was in the lead and would not give it up for the remainder of the race.

But his anxieties were not over. During the last 37 laps, there were three more caution periods, each one allowing Yarborough to close in on Elliott's bumper on each restart.

Without power steering, Yarborough was forced to drive a car which handled like a tank. "I had to use both arms, both hands, and both feet," said the man who has won five Southern 500s.

Yarborough's predicament was all Elliott needed. With his car handling far better than it had, his Thunderbird was too much for Yarborough. Elliott went on to win by two seconds.

"I would have really rather had no one to race," said Elliott, whose race winnings today totaled $53,725. "Racing the track here is hard enough. But at the end, I gave up racing the track itself and did what I had to do. Cale is tough, but he'll race you clean. As it was, I gave it my best shot, and I know he would have done the same."

Geoff Bodine emerged in third place in the Levi Garrett Monte Carlo while Neil Bonnett took fourth place in a Johnson/Budweiser Monte Carlo, one lap down. Ron Bouchard took fifth place, one lap down in the Beebe/Valvoline Buick, while Ricky Rudd took sixth place in the Moore/Motorcraft Thunderbird, also one lap down. Terry Labonte was seventh, two laps down in the Hagan/Piedmont Airlines Monte Carlo, Benny Parsons was eighth, two laps back in the Jackson/Copenhagen Monte Carlo, Joe Ruttman took ninth, three laps down in the Sheppard/Folgers Monte Carlo, and Kyle Petty rounded out the top 10, three laps down in the Wood Brothers/7-Eleven Thunderbird.

Engine failure sidelined David Pearson's Chattanooga Chew Thunderbird after just 17 laps, Rusty Wallace and Phil Parsons were eliminated in a wreck on the 22nd lap, engine failure claimed Bobby Allison's Miller American Thunderbird after 162 laps, A.J. Foyt retired his Copenhagen Oldsmobile with failed brakes after 248 laps and a broken brake caliper relegated Darrell Waltrip to 17th place, 12 laps in arrears.

The victory strengthened Elliott's hold on first place in the Winston Cup standings. He now has 3,176 points and leads Waltrip by 206 points with eight races remaining in 1985.

Asked how he felt after taking the checkered flag that assured him the $1 million and the victory, Elliott said, "Relieved."

"That's definite," he added. "There was a great deal of pressure on the team all week, and there was the pressure to keep the car together during the race. Anything could have happened. I could have run the car into the wall. But fortunately, everything worked out.

"I think everyone on the track gave me the benefit of the doubt. But they sure didn't wait on me. Those who could have won tried hard. Until something happened to him, I don't think I could have beaten Harry. When he was dialed in and wanted to go, he just went.

"It worked out that there was a bit of give and take, and that's the way it has to be on this track or you are not going to finish the race."

Elliott's win thrilled the capacity crowd of 68,000, which came to see the red-haired driver claim his big prize.

"With maybe 35-40 laps to go, I could see the crowd on its feet," said Elliott. "It seemed like everyone was tense and excited. They were all on their feet. I don't know if they ever sat down.

"As for me, well, I am going to celebrate by sitting down and resting. I want to spend some quiet time with my family. That will be our celebration, and then we'll work on the car for the next race at Richmond (Va.). I'm not going to worry about the championship. I am going to take each race as it comes and try to prepare the cars as best as possible. If something happens to 'em, we'll take 'em home and fix 'em."

Asked how he might summarize the day's historical event, Elliott said, "Ernie [his brother] and I talked on the radio after I won the race. We said to each other that we had done a good job and that somebody up there was looking out for us."

And indeed that is the way it was.

By Steve Waid

12

Crowd Pleaser

Earnhardt Puts On A Show In Yet Another Talladega Triumph

Dale Earnhardt was considered the master of the draft, a guy who could "see" the air. That was the biggest reason he did so well at NASCAR's restrictor-plate tracks, Daytona International Speedway and Talladega Superspeedway. Perhaps no better proof was provided than in the Winston 500. Running in 16th place with just six laps left, Earnhardt put on an exhibition of speed seldom seen. With just two laps remaining, he passed teammate Mike Skinner for the lead and then left any supposed challengers in the dust. Even today, people wonder just how did he do it? How could he come so far so fast? It was classic Earnhardt as he won the final race of his illustrious career.

—Steve Waid

Dale Earnhardt hates restrictor-plate racing. Always has. Always will. And that's not going to change no matter how many times he wins at NASCAR's biggest track.

The day before the Winston 500, he said they'd taken racing out of the drivers' hands here years ago when they first bolted carburetor plates on the cars. So the fact that NASCAR changed the size of the plate less than 24 hours before the race was something he could shrug off as just another reason to hate plate racing.

Yet the more he gripes about it, the more determined he seems to go out and prove himself wrong. In another trademark performance, Earnhardt maneuvered from 22nd to the lead in the final, frantic 10 laps on the way to his 10th career win at Talladega Superspeedway. If that's not the mark of a great driver, nothing is.

Earnhardt may not truly see the air as has long been discussed, but he sure can see the way to the front when it matters most.

Just don't ask how he got there. Or what he thinks of restrictor plates. Not even winning Winston's No Bull 5 $1 million bonus could change his opinion.

"I still don't like restrictor-plate racing," he said. "I'm not that good at it."

Well, if he ever gets to the level he considers proficient, the other 42 drivers ought to take the afternoon off. But if that happened, fans wouldn't know what to do at Daytona and Talladega. If Earnhardt's not leading, the most fun is watching his black Chevrolet to see how he gets to the front.

You pretty much have to watch for yourself. And you should probably take notes – or have the VCR running at home – because even Earnhardt had a hard time explaining exactly how he won for the 76th time in a legendary career. It was simply that spectacular.

One minute he was nowhere to be seen, up to just 16th with six laps left, then he was blowing by Richard Childress Racing teammate Mike Skinner with two laps remaining for the lead. He then outran drafting partners Kenny Wallace and Joe Nemechek to the stripe, while Skinner was shuffled to sixth behind Jeff Gordon and Terry Labonte.

Crew chief Kevin Hamlin, Earnhardt, and owner
Richard Childress share the post race spotlight.

DAVID CHOBAT PHOTO

"I don't know how I won it, honestly," Earnhardt said. "We had moved up and got pushed back again. I was up and down there between 10 and 15 (laps) to go. To be 18th or wherever we were with five to go is pretty impressive and says a lot for the rules and spotters and everything to make the racing more competitive. The problem is, it's hard to move through these cars. You've got to work your way around and by them.

"We just were fortunate to get hooked up with Kenny and Joe Nemechek there and work our way to the front. Basically, that's how I won the race, because Kenny and Joe got in there and all three Chevrolets got together and worked their way to the front."

Childress, Earnhardt and Andy Petree, who owns the cars of Wallace and Nemechek, have an engineering alliance to help the cars aerodynamically. But thoughts of being teammates in some broad sense played no role in the outcome. Wallace simply knew the best chance for his first Winston Cup win would come by working with Earnhardt on the way to the front.

That's why he kept bump-drafting with the seven-time champion.

"I had no choice but to hit him and keep pushing him into the lead," Wallace said. "... I was doing everything but hitting him through the trioval. I realized once I hit him I wasn't going to lift him. Sometimes you hit these guys and it lifts them up. I hit Earnhardt once square and I knocked the hell out of him three or four times and I personally won the race for him."

Earnhardt had help beyond that provided by Wallace and Nemechek, including some from his son. On a day when NASCAR's new aerodynamic rules helped produce 49 lead changes among 21 drivers, it appeared Earnhardt Jr. might post his third career win until John Andretti got by on lap 185. Skinner led the next circuit before

things got even crazier than normal.

Earnhardt Jr. tried getting a run on Skinner and got down on the apron alongside him before thinking better of the maneuver, which might have triggered a huge wreck had he forced the issue. Still, Skinner had to check up for an instant, which is when Earnhardt got back in front.

"Dad just got a great run on the outside," Earnhardt Jr. said. "Skinner was not going to win the race in the position he was in, so I either had to get by him or finish behind him."

Master that he is, Wallace and Nemechek simply couldn't make a move on Earnhardt, whose win was greeted with a rousing ovation from the faithful, many of whom rarely sat the entire day.

And while many were fans of the racing brought on by the new aero package, not all were smiling.

"It's 43 cars that look like they're in a parking lot," groused Frankie Stoddard, Jeff Burton's crew chief. "You could take a picture of the road that goes to Oxford, Ala. that's four lanes wide, and that would look exactly what it was like watching this race. Boring. Boring. Boring."

Considering Chevrolets swept the top six spots and Burton's Ford finished 29th after losing a lap to

a cut tire, Stoddard's sentiments are understandable. But it wasn't just the Ford contingent griping.

Jimmy Makar, crew chief for points leader Labonte, was rather displeased after his driver got shuffled back to 12th during the furious finish.

"It was exactly what we expected," Makar said. "(NASCAR) got what they wanted, a bunch of junk. We'd accomplish the same thing in a 10-lap or a 25-lap race here. It's all the same. It ain't about good race cars, it's about a chess match: who makes the right move, who makes the wrong move; who slips, who doesn't. That's what happened there at the end. Little E got down on the bottom, slipped, about wrecked, caused one line to slow up and the other line went, and that's all it took.

"It's not about racing to me here. It never has been since they've gone to this kind of restrictor plate racing. It's great for the fans, I know. It's a great show. But it's not much fun racing."

It was certainly harrowing at times, not to mention nostalgic. Dave Marcis led the second lap after starting ninth, Bill Elliott ran like it was 1988 and Ken Schrader had moments where it looked like he might earn his first Cup win since 1991. Cars were running three- and sometimes four-wide with

Earnhardt "helps" crew chief Kevin Hamlin enjoy a little bubbly.
DAVID CHOBAT PHOTO

abandon and you just kept waiting for the huge crash that usually punctuates affairs at Daytona and Talladega.

Instead, the race was slowed by just three cautions as Earnhardt averaged 165.681 mph. And the biggest wreck, involving five cars, came after those on the lead lap had taken the checkered flag. By then, Earnhardt's crew was celebrating, though it was a mild-mannered affair for crew chief Kevin Hamlin, who injured his back a night earlier while driving a Monster Truck.

With many drivers privately predicting a wreckfest prior to the event, Earnhardt and Wallace were among those pleasantly surprised.

"I can't say enough about the way they worked together," Earnhardt said. "I've got to hand it to the drivers. ... I know there at the end they got a little antsy, a little bumping and a little bit of rubbing. I know they wrecked there at the start-finish line. They were going for it, but it was a pretty good day seeing that kind of racing."

"It was a deal where we said, if anybody goes underneath the yellow line all day long, we're going to name them idiots," Wallace said. "Then, with five

to go, we said, if you want to be an idiot, it's OK."

For the most part, though, everyone kept their heads. A number of drivers complained of being worn out physically and mentally afterwards, but Earnhardt, not surprisingly, had a spring in his step. In fact, he even did a little jig for fans gathered outside the press box, where Earnhardt traveled for his post-race interview.

"They need to work out, don't they?" he asked. "I'm pretty relaxed. It was a good race for me, my car drove good all day. It just worked well. I didn't get tired or burned out during the day. I really felt great after the race. I was excited about the win. I seemed to be more relaxed than usual. And I still am. I'm not a bit tired. I don't feel like I raced at all today from the way I feel."

Earnhardt was even charitable enough to commend NASCAR for

taking chances by changing the aero rules in an attempt to create better racing at Daytona in 2001. Still, he wasn't about to let them completely off the hook.

"It was a good race," he said. "But I think you'd have seen just as good a race with the other (bigger) plate, too. ... They made a change, it worked. ... It's not easy for anybody to make a call like that. It's a big responsibility. I think they did a good job with it. I don't like restrictor-plate racing. But they made a call and stuck by their guns. You have to support them for that."

If the cars are equipped with parachutes next year, it probably won't slow Earnhardt. But whatever he does here next, he'll have a hard time topping this performance.

"Coming from the back to (win), I can't compare this one with any race I've won on that kind of scale," he said. "To come back and pass on the white-flag lap, take the lead and win the race is pretty awesome. It's one of the great, if not the greatest, Talladega races I've probably ever run."

Or as Wallace said of his run to the front with Earnhardt: "That was Earnhardt and Talladega." 🏁

By Mark Ashenfelter

2000 Winston 500 Top Ten

Finish	Start	No.	Driver	Team/Owner	Laps	Money
1	20	3	Dale Earnhardt	RCR	188	$135,900
2	7	55	Kenny Wallace	Andy Petree Racing	188	98,170
3	1	33	Joe Nemechek	Andy Petree Racing	188	85,685
4	8	24	Jeff Gordon	Hendrick Motorsports	188	82,100
5	17	5	Terry Labonte	Hendrick Motorsports	188	73,700
6	24	31	Mike Skinner	RCR	188	62,450
7	27	6	Mark Martin	Roush Racing	188	62,350
8	38	2	Rusty Wallace	Penske Racing South	188	59,500
9	43	27	Mike Bliss	Eel River Racing	188	46,700
10	36	17	Matt Kenseth	Roush Racing	188	65,100

Time of Race: 3 hours, 1 minute, 6 seconds
Pole Winner: Joe Nemechek – 190.279 mph
Average Speed: 165.681 mph
Cautions: 3 for 13 laps
Margin of Victory: 0.119 second
Attendance: 140,000

Having scorched his way from 16th to first in just six laps, Earnhardt has a lot to celebrate.

DAVID CHOBAT PHOTO

1999 Goody's Headache Powder 500

Bristol Motor Speedway
Bristol, Tennessee
August 28, 1999

13

'Ironhead' vs. 'Iron Man'

Earnhardt Pushes Way To Controversial Last-Lap Win At Bristol

Fans who go to races at Bristol Motor Speedway know what to expect – beatin', bangin', crunched sheet metal and flaring tempers. They got that by a bushel load in the Goody's 500. Terry Labonte was leading on the final lap, but along came Dale Earnhardt – hailed by many and vilified by just as many for employing any and all tactics necessary to win. Earnhardt popped Labonte between turns one and two, spun him, and went on to win the race. You can just imagine the reaction from the Labonte camp, but it went much further than that. Other competitors were just as angry, and most of the 145,000 fans on hand expressed their discontent with boos, gestures and obscenities.

—Steve Waid

Surreal. Absolutely surreal. Wrecked race cars littered across the track as the checkered flag flies, outrageous controversy, screaming and finger-flipping fans teetering on the edge of delirium, angry race teams and a race no one will soon forget.

In other words, just another typical August Saturday night at Bristol Motor Speedway, deja vu all over again.

Tempers run hot and out of control at the high-banked 0.533-mile Bristol pressure cooker, a place where you damn well better be ready to fight if you come.

And in the entire half century history of NASCAR, you can make a pretty compelling case that no one's ever spoiled for a fight more than seven-time champion Dale Earnhardt.

Call him "The Man In Black," "The Intimidator," "Ironhead" or what you choose, no one has a stronger will to win than Earnhardt. And while some were ready to dismiss the 48-year-old, Kannapolis, N.C., native as being over the hill after a winless 1997 season and just one victory last year, Earnhardt

proved he's far from finished at this year's running of the Goody's Headache Powder 500 in Bristol.

In fact, Earnhardt laid waste to the old adage about not teaching old dogs new tricks, 'cause he sure learned an important one here: You can't win wrecking Terry Labonte in the last turn of the last lap, as he did in 1995. To win, you've got to wreck him in the first turn of the last lap.

Four years ago at Bristol, Earnhardt rammed the back of Labonte coming out of turn four, but the Texan's mangled Hendrick Motorsports Chevrolet still managed to slide across the finish line first with Earnhardt second.

This time was different. Tonight, before God, country, a full moon and 141,000 fired up race fans, Earnhardt again popped Labonte, this time between turns one and two of lap 500, igniting a firestorm of rage among rivals and race fans alike and relegating Labonte to eighth, after he had made a miraculous late charge and seemed certain of victory.

Finishing between the victorious Earnhardt and the vanquished Labonte were Jimmy Spencer, Ricky Rudd, Jeff Gordon,

The celebration erupts . . .

Tony Stewart, Mark Martin and Sterling Marlin in seventh. Rounding out the top 10 were Ward Burton and Ken Schrader.

It was Earnhardt's second win of the season, ninth at Bristol and 73rd of his illustrious career. And while Earnhardt and the Richard Childress Racing team were happy, few others were. The fans roared their collective discontent, ringing the track with obscenities, upraised middle fingers and choruses of boos. Many competitors were angry afterward as well.

"It wasn't right. It wasn't right," second-place finisher Jimmy Spencer said of Earnhardt's rough-house tactics. Spencer, himself no stranger to aggressive driving, said, "I used to fight for stuff worse than that on Saturday nights."

"To tell you the truth, I knew there was going to be a wreck," added Rudd. " ... In that situation, you've got to look at who you're dealing with."

Earnhardt, as you might expect, was unapologetic.

"If it comes down to the last lap and you're going for it and you get into somebody, you get into them. You don't mean to, but you mean to race them."

The chaotic finish led NASCAR officials to huddle for more than hour before letting the victory stand.

Well after midnight, NASCAR Chief Operating Officer Mike Helton stood outside the NASCAR trailer trying to explain why Earnhardt's victory was allowed to stand despite the hard contact that sent Labonte into the wall.

"After seeing the end of the race and reviewing all of the tapes, NASCAR is going to let the finish order stand as it completed," Helton said.

"Naturally it would have been better had the race finished under different circumstances, but inasmuch as in having to make a decision whether or not you take a race away from someone for something that happens on the race track, the information that you have or the result is, you have

to be very inconclusive and be certain about that. And in this case it's not inconclusive that it was a racing accident on the way back to the checkered flag. And therefore we're going to leave the standings the way they were at the finish of the race.

"If there were going to be any actions taken, they would have been taken tonight. Whether or not NASCAR takes a look at future steps to avoid these types of incidents in the past that are not clearly handled, we may take a look at that, but tonight's results will stand the way they are."

Earnhardt, who has seen both sides of bump-and-run moves over the years, shrugged off the criticism.

"I've always just took my medicine, took what happened and just sucked it up and just go to the next race. You can't change or do anything about it," he said.

Labonte, naturally was unimpressed.

"I won't even waste my time to go to the (NASCAR) trailer and talk to them about it. I've been there before."

And he was none too subtle about giving Earnhardt a payback.

"He better tighten his belts," warned Labonte.

It didn't take long for the action to heat up. Second-qualifier Rusty Wallace grabbed the lead from pole-sitter Stewart at the start, powering around the outside of the Joe Gibbs Racing Pontiac when the green flag dropped.

Hapless Robert Pressley was the first casualty of the Saturday night bullring madness, wrecking his Jasper Motorsports Ford between turns one and two on lap three to bring out the first caution of the night.

Although he lost the lead at the start, Stewart hounded Wallace and on lap 22 popped him in the rear bumper between turns three and four just to let him know he was still there.

On lap 27, Stewart finally made it by Wallace, taking over the point off of turn two, a move Gordon would repeat a lap later to drop Wallace to third place.

Up front, Stewart held on comfortably, with the order of the top three staying the same for the next 50 laps.

Then came the first key moment of the race.

On lap 78 points leader Dale Jarrett got squirrelly off of turn two, and as the parade of Cup cars made their way to three, all hell broke loose as Jarrett spun and collected John Andretti, Hut Stricklin, Michael Waltrip, Bill Elliott, Jeremy Mayfield and Bobby Hamilton.

Although Jarrett suffered only right side damage, the worst was yet to come.

Jerry Nadeau, who was subbing for the injured Ernie Irvan in the MB2 Motorsports Pontiac, tagged the back of Jarrett's Ford on the frontstretch, bringing out another yellow flag and sending the Robert Yates Racing Ford into the pits

Earnhardt, with wife Teresa, poses for pictures in victory lane.
DAVID CHOBAT PHOTO

for lengthy repairs that would take 155 laps.

Jarrett, who began the night with a seemingly unassailable 300-point lead over Mark Martin in the Winston Cup championship, saw his margin dwindle to a still-comfortable 213 points by the end of the race.

To his credit, Jarrett took responsibility for the first wreck.

"I created the problem for some other people and myself," Jarrett said. "It was my fault."

NASCAR, however, penalized Nadeau two laps for rough driving, which did not go over well with his team and crew chief Ryan Pemberton.

"Where's the justice at?" Pemberton asked after the race. "What the 3 car did, that was blatant. I don't know, that was at least two laps, I think."

As the night wore on, rookie Stewart set the pace, leading a race-high 225 laps. But before long, the usual Bristol hijinks started to play out.

David Green hit the turn-three wall midway through the race to bring out the yellow flag again. When the leaders all pitted on lap 252, it was Gordon out first, then Martin, Stewart, Marlin and Bobby Labonte.

Ten laps later, Kyle Petty tapped Stricklin coming out of turn four, an accident that also snared Johnny Benson.

The track went green on lap 269, and five laps later Earnhardt and Rusty Wallace had contact, causing Wallace's left rear to go down. Wallace pitted for fresh rubber on lap 278, but he was two laps down and effectively out of contention for a win.

It got worse. Chad Little spun Mayfield and collected Kenny Irwin and Wally Dallenbach in turn two on lap 290.

The green flew again on lap 296, and on the restart Stewart almost lost it in turn one as he went high, allowing Martin to retake second place.

Then Irwin brought out yet another yellow flag, getting loose into Nadeau in turn four, and wrecking half a dozen other cars in the process.

With the yellow out, the complexion of the race changed.

About half of the lead-lap car pitted on lap 300, but when the green flag came back out on lap 305, the order was jumbled by the cars that stayed out: Terry Labonte ahead of Earnhardt, Spencer, Geoffrey Bodine, Rudd, Gordon, Bobby Labonte, Stewart Martin and Marlin.

Stewart's decision to pit proved to be a good one: His right rear tire was going flat.

Then the race settled down, with veterans Labonte and Earnhardt in command out front, which is how it stayed for the final 200 laps, as they swapped the lead seven more times.

Dave Marcis slowed high on the track on lap 411, after he couldn't get an opening down low to pit. The track went yellow and NASCAR assessed Marcis a one-lap penalty for intentionally bringing out a caution.

The leaders all pitted on lap 412, with Labonte emerging ahead of teammate Gordon, Earnhardt, Stewart, Bobby Labonte, Martin, Rudd, Spencer, Little and Brett Bodine.

Labonte remained in the lead until lap 435, when Earnhardt passed him and stayed in front for four laps, before Labonte went back into the lead, a position he would hold onto until the 490th of 500 laps.

The final 10 laps were pure bedlam. Mayfield and Wally Dallenbach collided on the backstretch on lap 490, as the leaders rushed by. Labonte made it safely into turn three when he was spun by Darrell Waltrip.

"I don't know what he was thinking," a peeved Labonte said afterward.

Labonte ducked into the pits for fresh tires and seemed out of it. But with few cars left on the lead lap, he emerged from the pits fifth behind Earnhardt, Stewart, Gordon – none of whom had pitted – and Martin.

When the green flag came out again on lap 496, Labonte took off like a shot on his fresh tires, quickly passing the three cars ahead of him, Martin first, then on lap 498 getting by Gordon and Stewart, respectively.

On lap 499 he muscled past Earnhardt, bumping him a little in turns three and four. It appeared certain he was headed for victory lane. At least until Earnhardt nailed him on the last lap, that is.

"I don't think I spun Terry intentionally," Earnhardt said. "You'll have to go to NASCAR about all that. I've got big shoulders and I can take the pressure or the blame or whatever. It was not an intentional bump, but it happened.

"I'm sure we'll hear about the race for awhile, and we'll just have to take it like it is. Like I said, I have broad shoulders. I have to take what comes and race from here on.

"If it would have been on the other foot and I'd been the one turned around, I would think about it pretty hard and know he was going to race me hard to win."

John Hendrick argued driver Labonte's case afterward in the NASCAR trailer, but to no avail.

"They made their ruling, they're not going to change anything," said Hendrick. "It stands. We're not happy with it at all. Everybody saw what happened. It's a shame for Terry 'cause he fought back so hard."

Runner-up Spencer, however, may have had the definitive word on the last-lap melee.

"I went into the final turn, and wow, Ironman and Ironhead got together," he said.

And that was that. 🏁

By Tom Jensen

Even amid the controversy of a last lap bumpin-pass, Kevin Hamlin, Earnhardt, and Richard Childress are all smiles in victory lane.

2000 Winston 500 Top Ten

Finish	Start	No.	Driver	Team/Owner	Laps	Money
1	26	3	Dale Earnhardt	RCR	500	$89,880
2	24	23	Jimmy Spencer	Travis Carter Enterp.	500	76,265
3	35	10	Ricky Rudd	Rudd Perf. Mtsp.	500	64,190
4	4	24	Jeff Gordon	Hendrick Motorsports	500	71,505
5	1	20	Tony Stewart	Joe Gibbs Racing	500	64,915
6	7	6	Mark Martin	Roush Racing	500	48,165
7	10	40	Sterling Marlin	Team Sabco	500	42,840
8	9	5	Terry Labonte	Hendrick Motorsports	499	58,615
9	5	22	Ward Burton	Bill Davis Racing	499	41,915
10	13	33	Ken Schrader	Andy Petree Racing	499	47,005

Time of Race: 2 hours, 55 minutes, 11 seconds
Pole Winner: Tony Stewart – 124.589 mph
Average Speed: 91.276 mph
Cautions: 10 for 60 laps
Margin of Victory: 0.189 second
Attendance: 145,000

Charlotte Motor Speedway
Charlotte, North Carolina
May 16, 1992

14

Allison Wins In Slam-Bang Affair

Takes Checkered Flag Then Impacts With Wall In Wildest Finish Ever

The Winston was highly anticipated for one reason: It would be the first superspeedway race held at night, under the bright lights at Charlotte Motor Speedway. It turned out to be a thriller. On the last lap, Kyle Petty, Dale Earnhardt and Davey Allison were racing for the win. Petty and Earnhardt went side by side in turn three, and Earnhardt was sent into a spin. Allison moved inside Petty out of the fourth turn. The leaders bounced off each other and amid sparks, Allison slid sideways across the finish line – and into the wall. He never got to celebrate the victory. He was taken to a hospital for observation but raced again the next week.

—Steve Waid

Under the full moon, predictably weird things happen and, indeed they did.

On the last lap of The Winston, there were not one, but two incidents that affected the outcome of NASCAR Winston Cup's "all-star" race. As a result, Davey Allison forged his second-straight victory in the event in dramatic fashion over a determined Kyle Petty.

But Allison wasn't around to enjoy a victory lane celebration.

Because of a race-closing, pulse-pounding finish with Petty that ended with Allison's Robert Yates Racing Ford crashing into the wall on the frontstretch beyond the finish line, a banged-up Allison was transported via helicopter to Carolinas Medical Center in Charlotte, N.C.

The race winner was listed as conscious, alert and in satisfactory condition. He was scheduled to undergo tests for what was reported to be a "banged-up" leg.

Meanwhile, it was up to team owner Robert Yates to take the rewards of triumph in victory lane. Even the bashed Ford nicknamed "007", which claimed its fourth triumph in its last five starts at CMS, wasn't there.

Despite all of this, Allison could be satisfied with several achievements. He joined Dale Earnhardt as the only drivers to have won The Winston twice. By virtue of his pole triumph, his victory in the first 30-lap segment of The Winston and his ultimate triumph in the closing 10-lap "shootout," he earned a whopping $300,000, which boosted his season earnings to $885,160.

Allison also saw his status as the season's most dominant driver improve. He has three Winston Cup victories already this season and now, The Winston. He will be the heavy favorite to win the Coca-Cola 600 at CMS on May 24, a victory which would earn him a $1 million bonus through The Winston Million.

A wild ride. Allison crosses the finish line just ahead of Kyle Petty, who bumps Allison and sends him spinning.

DAVID CHOBAT PHOTO (4)

In The Winston, Allison literally went from first to last to first. Starting No. 1 for the first 30-lap segment, he was never seriously challenged and went on to win by 0.94 second over Bill Elliott, driver of the Junior Johnson & Associates Ford. That earned him a cool $50,000.

After a 10-minute break during which the teams did routine work on their cars, Allison restarted at the rear of the field. An inverted start won the vote of fans easily – 8,475 to 609 – and the task of the 31-year-old Hueytown, Ala., resident would be to thread his way through a strongly competitive field.

For a time, it appeared he would be in trouble. With Geoff Bodine in the Bud Moore Engineering Ford pacing the field early in the segment Allison was able to make up little distance.

Meanwhile, Petty, in the SabCo Racing Pontiac, took charge. He breezed by Bodine on lap 38. One lap later, Dale Earnhardt put his RCR Enterprises Chevrolet in second place, six car lengths in arrears.

By Lap 42, Ernie Irvan had put his Morgan-McClure Chevrolet into second place but Petty continued to hold sway – easily. He won the second segment by nearly two seconds over Irvan, with Earnhardt in third.

Allison, meanwhile, had moved up to sixth place. When the final 10-lap "shootout" began after a delay of four caution laps – none of which counted – he would be in position to win.

The question was, could he?

When the last laps began, Petty quickly pulled away. On lap 62, Earnhardt dispatched Irvan and took over second place, nearly a second behind Petty. A classic confrontation seemed in order.

It was certain on lap 63, when Darrell Waltrip took a wild ride through the grass on the frontstretch and then spun to the inside of the first turn to bring out a caution. Although the caution

laps would not count, the field would be bunched up, two abreast, for the restart.

Petty did not need the caution. With seven laps left in the race, he would restart with Earnhardt alongside him and Allison, who had made up two positions, at his rear.

Sure enough, Earnhardt snatched the lead before the field had completed two laps. If that wasn't enough, Allison put Petty in third place as the cars roared down the backstretch.

But this was The Winston, where things can change quickly and inexplicably – especially under a full moon.

1992 The Winston Top Ten

Finish	Start	No.	Driver	Team/Owner	Laps	Money
1	1	28	Davey Allison	Robert Yates Racing	70	$300,000
2	16	42	Kyle Petty	SabCo Racing	70	130,000
3	4	25	Ken Schrader	Hendrick Motorsports	70	50,000
4	9	5	Ricky Rudd	Hendrick Motorsports	70	30,000
5	3	11	Bill Elliott	Junior Johnson	70	47,000
6	2	2	Rusty Wallace	Roger Penske	70	42,500
7	14	7	Alan Kulwicki	AK Racing	70	23,000
8	17	4	Ernie Irvan	Morgan-McClure	70	31,500
9	15	43	Richard Petty	Petty Enterprises	70	20,500
10	13	94	Terry Labonte	Billy Hagan	70	19,500

Time of Race: 47 minutes, 29 seconds
Pole Winner: Davey Allison – 135.265 mph (including 11.19-second pit stop)
Average Speed: 132.678 mph
Cautions: 1 for 5 laps
Margin of Victory: 4 feet
Attendance: 133,500

On lap 66, Petty took second place away from Allison, and it appeared Earnhardt and Petty would fight it out to see who would give General Motors its first win of 1992.

On the last lap, everything changed. Earnhardt charged into turn three with Petty glued to his bumper. Allison wasn't far behind. Then Earnhardt broke loose between turns three and four, sliding toward the outside wall in a scene reminiscent of 1989, when Darrell Waltrip spun after contact with Rusty Wallace, who went on to win that year.

Petty's path to victory, though, was by no means clear. The incident had forced him to ease up to help gain control of his car. As he did so, Allison, who never backed off, charged forward and found himself locked alongside Petty as the two came out of the fourth turn.

There was a bump…then another.

With Allison to Petty's inside, the shoving match continued as they approached the finish line rapidly.

Allison gained the edge. He was being pinched to the grass by Petty but held on and took the checkered flag by a half-car length.

But the action wasn't over. One last contact between Allison and Petty sent Allison's car looping around the front end of Petty's Pontiac. Out of control and in a smoking slide, Allison slammed into the retaining wall and then bounced into the grass in the infield at the end of the frontstretch dogleg.

Safety crews – in fact, his own Yates crew – sped toward Allison immediately after his Ford came to a halt. Concern was raised as word spread that Allison was unconscious and sheet metal had to be cut away from the car roof to retrieve him.

An ambulance came on the scene, and a stretcher was readied. Finally, Allison was removed from the car. He had been fitted with a neck brace, but nearly all concern of a serious injury disappeared as he waved to the crowd.

Although there was a brief debate over whether Allison would report to victory lane, it was decided to transport him to the hospital to check his injured leg – it wasn't broken – and to conduct a CAT scan.

Allison didn't get the cheers in victory lane, but the grandstands applauded lustily as the helicopter rose and flew off.

The fact was Allison didn't know he had won the race until he was visited in the infield care center by Yates and crew chief Larry McReynolds. He woozily asked, "Well, boys, what happened?" And he was told.

A late report from Carolinas Medical Center said Allison had been removed from the trauma unit and was in stable condition. He had suffered a bruised lung, bruised legs and a concussion. He was scheduled to undergo more tests to determine the severity of his injuries.

Ken Schrader, who had finished second in three straight The Winstons, took third this time in the Hendrick Motorsports Chevrolet. Teammate Ricky Rudd was fourth in another Chevrolet while Bill Elliott rounded out the top five.

Sixth place went to Rusty Wallace in the Penske Racing South Pontiac, seventh to Alan Kulwicki in the Kulwicki Racing Ford, eighth to Irvan, ninth to Richard Petty in the Petty Enterprises Pontiac, and Terry Labonte took 10th in the Hagan Racing Oldsmobile.

Dale Jarrett's smoking Chevrolet broke loose in the second turn on the third lap and caused a multicar accident which eventually eliminated Morgan Shepherd and Hut Stricklin, who, along with Dave Mader, were the only retirees of the race.

It's likely Allison's memory of his dramatic win will come only from what others tell him. Be that as it may, the record will show he did indeed win what many have already declared to be the most exciting, dramatic The Winston ever run.

By Steve Waid

Daytona International Speedway
Daytona Beach, Florida
February 14, 1988

15 Allison Caps Big Week With Daytona 500 Win

Bobby Allison Wins In Father-Son Finale

Bobby Allison had raced almost his entire adult life. So it was that his son Davey wanted to follow in his footsteps. Davey was NASCAR's Rookie of the Year in 1987 and had already won twice as the '88 Daytona 500 loomed. One of Davey's biggest dreams was to be racing his father for a victory. He got it, but it didn't end the way he wished. In the lead, Bobby held off many challenges from his son over the closing laps to win the race for the third time in his career. Bobby said afterward that his feelings about beating one of the sport's future stars were hard to put into words.

—Steve Waid

In his 22 years of steady NASCAR Winston Cup competition, Bobby Allison has many fond memories of Daytona International Speedway. But it is quite possible the 1988 Daytona 500 NASCAR Winston Cup race will head his list of treasured recollections.

By winning the classic race on the 2.5-mile Daytona track, the 50-year-old Allison established records, enhanced his position as one of NASCAR's premier drivers and completed Speed Weeks with an account of success seldom compiled by any competitor.

The victory was Allison's third in the Daytona 500, his last coming in 1982. He has now won 16 times at Daytona, making him the all-time winningest driver and breaking him out of a tie with Cale Yarborough. He also moved ahead of Yarborough into third place on NASCAR's all-time winners' list with 84.

The Daytona 500 was Allison's third win in four days at the track. He also won a 125-mile qualifying race on Feb. 11 and

the Goody's 300 Busch Series race on Feb. 13. In the Feb. 7 Busch Clash, he logged a third-place finish.

Further, Allison gave General Motors' squad of "new" cars a victory as he won in a Stavola/Miller American Buick Regal prepared in the team's shop in Harrisburg, N.C.

But all of that is probably secondary to the emotional charge Allison must have felt as he battled his 26-year-old son, Davey, for the win. Davey, in the Ranier/Havoline Ford Thunderbird, was the only other competitor who had a remote chance of upending the elder Allison over the race's final few laps.

Although he didn't do it, he made a noble effort, putting his car under his father's as the two came around the third and fourth turns on the final lap. He finished second by two and one-half car lengths.

"It was really good to be in front," said Bobby Allison. "It was a great feeling to look back and see somebody you think is the best coming up and know it is your own son. It is a very special

It's a family affair. Son Davey showers father Bobby with congratulations . . . and beer.

feeling, and it is hard to put into words."

"I've got mixed emotions," said Davey. "I had a lot of dreams when I was growing up. And one of them was to be battling my dad to the wire in a race. The only difference is I wanted to finish first."

The Allisons became the first father-son combination to sweep the top two positions in a NASCAR Winston Cup – formerly Grand National – event since Lee Petty beat son Richard at Heidelberg Raceway in Pittsburgh on July 10, 1960.

After his victories in the qualifier and the Goody's 300, Allison was listed as a strong favorite to win the Daytona 500. His Buick was as powerful as predicted as Allison led seven times for 70 laps, tops among all competitors and one more than Darrell Waltrip in the Hendrick/Tide Chevrolet Monte Carlo SS.

Among the contenders all day, Bobby Allison moved into second place with his son in tow on lap 152 and then snatched the lead from Waltrip on lap 155. Four laps later, Davey moved into second place, and the trio of the Allisons and Waltrip opened up a 4.16-second margin on a pack led by Buddy Baker in the Red Baron Pizza Oldsmobile Cutlass and Dale Earnhardt in the Childress/GM Goodwrench Chevrolet.

On lap 162, Bobby gave way to his son when he pitted for gas and began a stream of green-flag pit stops. Davey followed on lap 164. So did the rest of the leaders save Waltrip, who remained on the track until lap 176 and had built up a 36-second margin on the field. Waltrip spent 10 seconds in the pits getting fuel.

Asked if he was worried Waltrip's margin might be too much to overcome, Bobby Allison said, "We got the information that when he came out of the pits he would be five or six seconds ahead of us. Davey and I were hooked up in a draft, and we were making up five to six-tenths of a second on him, so

I have no doubt we would have caught him."

The matter became academic on lap 177, when Harry Gant brought out the race's sixth caution flag when he crashed in the second turn. After another series of pit stops, the race was restarted on lap 183 with Phil Parsons in the Crown/Skoal Classic Oldsmobile the leader. Davey Allison followed, then Waltrip and Bobby Allison.

Before the lap was completed, Bobby Allison had moved into the lead with Davey right behind him. Then, on lap 185, something gave out in Waltrip's engine, and he quickly faded, losing the five-car lead draft.

Debris on the track brought out the seventh and final caution flag on lap 188, but two laps later, the race resumed with a tight five-car pack consisting of the Allisons, Baker, Parsons and Terry Labonte leading the way. Waltrip hovered back in 11th place.

On lap 192, Baker moved into second place in the third turn, but Davey Allison quickly moved alongside him to retake the position. Caught outside the draft, Baker drifted to eighth place.

Just four laps from the finish of the 200-lap race, a 13-car draft was formed, but Bobby Allison's point position wasn't challenged until the last lap. Between turns three and four, Davey took the low route, and while he pulled within striking distance of his father, he could not pass. His father led the final 18 laps.

"I knew my best bet was to help Dad get away far enough so I could protect second place and make a move if I could," said Davey. "I knew he had been watching how I passed everyone earlier. He knew my car was working really well on the outside, so there was no way he would give up the outside line. That's why he was up there in between turns three and four.

"So I tried to fake that I was going high and get under him. I knew if I was successful, the only way

I was going to win was by a few inches."

"I think the reason I went up front as often as I could was my impression that my car was the best one left," said Bobby Allison, whose victory was worth $202,940. "Darrell was strong, but I felt I was slightly stronger. Then something happened to him and he faded. So my impression was to get the lead and not get hung up with someone in a fairly good car and get the sheet metal bent up.

"I saw the nose of Davey's car out of the corner of my eye, but I thought I had enough suds to beat him."

Asked if he had any concern he would become involved in a race-ending mishap with his father as the two battled for the lead, Davey Allison said, "I grew up working with this guy and I know how fair he is on the track. If my car could beat his, then it would. But he would make it very tough on me. He would never wreck me."

"Throughout my career I've tried to play it straight," Bobby Allison said. "And racing against

Bobby Allison enjoys his third Daytona 500 trophy.
DOZIER MOBLEY PHOTO

the best youngster to come along, I wouldn't do it any other way."

Parsons came home third for his best career finish while Neil Bonnett took fourth in the Rahmoc/Valvoline Pontiac Grand Prix. Terry Labonte rounded out the top five in the Johnson/Budweiser Chevrolet, meaning the top five finishing positions were occupied by five different car makes.

The race was marred by one serious multicar accident which took place on lap 106 and brought out the fourth caution period of the day. Richard Petty's STP Pontiac broke loose in the fourth turn and was clipped by A.J. Foyt's Copenhagen

1988 Daytona 500 Top Ten

Finish	Start	No.	Driver	Team/Owner	Laps	Money
1	3	12	Bobby Allison	Stavola Brothers	200	$202,940
2	2	28	Davey Allison	Ranier Racing	200	113,760
3	19	55	Phil Parsons	Jackson Brothers	200	81,625
4	14	75	Neil Bonnett	RahMoc	200	67,290
5	8	11	Terry Labonte	Junior Johnson	200	62,415
6	1	25	Ken Schrader	Hendrick Motorsports	200	72,215
7	5	27	Rusty Wallace	Blue Max Racing	200	59,990
8	12	44	Sterling Marlin	Billy Hagan	200	43,765
9	18	88	Buddy Baker	Baker-Schiff Racing	200	36,490
10	6	3	Dale Earnhardt	RCR Enterprises	200	52,540

Time of Race: 3 hours, 38 minutes, 8 seconds
Pole Winner: Ken Schrader – 193.823 mph
Average Speed: 137.531 mph
Cautions: 7 for 42 laps
Margin of Victory: 2 car lengths
Attendance: 140,000

Oldsmobile and Phil Barkdoll's Helen Rae Special Ford. Petty's car got airborne and then completed six barrel rolls near and against the outside wall before coming to a halt at the start of the front trioval. The rear end of the car shredded apart against the wall.

Cars shot in all directions around Petty's mass of mangled metal but the Crisco/Motorcraft Ford

couldn't avoid making contact, slamming into Petty one last time. Damaged in the incident were the cars of Bodine, Foyt, Rusty Wallace, Alan Kulwicki, Phil Barkdoll and Eddie Bierschwale. Of the group, Barkdoll, Foyt and Bodine retired. None of the drivers were injured.

After witnessing the nerve-shaking spectacle, many observers figured Petty was seriously injured – or worse. However, after reporting to Halifax Medical Center for treatment of a possible concussion and a sore right ankle, Petty was released.

The race continued for 20 laps at a crawl while crews replaced two fenceposts and retightened the safety cable on the front grandstand fence at the trioval. That contributed to the race's average speed of 137.531 mph – slowest for the Daytona 500 since 1960; when Junior Johnson won at 124.740 mph.

Other incidents included Connie Saylor's wreck in the fourth turn, which created the second yellow-flag period, and Cale Yarborough's spin in turn four, which produced caution period No. 3. Derrike Cope spun in the second turn on lap 177 to force yellow flag number five, after which came Gant's spin in the same location.

With 25 lead changes among 12 drivers, the race was more competitive than many had anticipated. During the week, it became evident that the Winston Cup cars equipped with the one-inch carburetor restrictor plates mandated by NASCAR at Daytona and Talladega, Ala., performed equally and passing could only be done if one car pulled out of the draft to help another. Further, Allison said after his win in the Goody's 300 that drivers were becoming involved in incidents because they showed "disrespect" for speed and position.

That didn't seem to be the case in the Daytona 500, however.

"There was a lot of beating and banging, but I think there were also a couple of important differences," Bobby said. "Two things happened. People showed more respect than they did earlier in the week and they learned how to cope with what we had to do. They learned how to run side by side out there and maybe experience some bent metal without ending up in a lump in the infield."

The elder Allison allowed that three wins at one track visit was the most he had accomplished in Winston Cup competition.

"I did have a double at Talladega in 1971 and at Charlotte (N.C.) one other time," he said. "It's just a big thrill for me, and it hasn't taken a toll at all.

"I think of things in threes. I won the qualifier and the Goody's 300, but then I had also won the boat for winning the 'fish off' in the fishing tournament they have at the infield lake here. I caught a giant fish. It was the largemouth bass and the largest thing about it was its mouth.

"So going into today's race, that had me a bit concerned."

But he didn't race like it. He raced like he always has for three hours, 38 minutes and eight seconds.

"You always have to have support, and on this team, I have it," he said. "With the Stavola brothers, Ron Puryear (team manager) and Jimmy Fennig (crew chief) and the crew, it makes for the kind of team you need to win. I've been with teams in the past that weren't like that, and when there was a poor performance, occasionally it was blamed on the driver.

"I guess this just proves I'm a late bloomer."

"I think it proves he's a winner," said Davey Allison. And he should know.

By Steve Waid

Elliott Roars Back To Victory Lane

Chalk Up Another For Elliott

Bill Elliott had a brilliant '85 season with 11 superspeedway victories. But none was more impressive than in the Winston 500 at Talladega Superspeedway. After losing two laps early because of a loose oil line, Elliott made up both without the benefit of caution periods and went on to run away with the victory. It was an exhibition of sheer speed. Elliott ran laps consistently over 200 mph. At Talladega, a driver isn't supposed to make up two lost laps without assistance from caution periods. But Elliott did it and in so doing, he left his rivals scratching their heads as they wondered just what it was he had under his hood.

—Steve Waid

There was a problem or two along the way, but Bill Elliott easily overcame them and did the expected: He showed the power of sheer speed and ran away with the Winston 500 NASCAR Winston Cup race today at Alabama International Motor Speedway.

Flaunting the strength of his Coors/Melling Ford Thunderbird, Elliott lost nearly two laps early in the race because of a loose oil line, made it up under the green and then went on to beat Kyle Petty to the finish line by a comfortable two seconds.

The victory was Elliott's fourth in five superspeedway races this season. He has now won six of the last nine, dating back to 1984.

This win, however, was significant in that it gave the Dawsonville, Ga., driver victories in two of the four events which make up the "Winston Million." That was worth $100,000 to Elliott, and should he win either the May 26 World 600 at Charlotte, N.C., or the Sept. 1 Southern 500 at Darlington, S.C., he will receive $1 million from R.J. Reynolds Tobacco Co.

"Winston is going to work me to death," said Elliott jokingly. "I dread the couple of weeks going into Charlotte. Yeah, the pressure is there. We might have won $100,000 today, but we're looking at $900,000 more."

The 500-mile race on the high banks of the 2.66-mile AIMS track was slowed just twice for eight laps by caution flags, allowing Elliott to win with an average speed of 186.288 mph. That broke the record for the fastest 500-mile auto race ever run, beating the old mark of 177.602 mph set by Buddy Baker in the 1980 Daytona 500.

Most observers felt the race would be fast in light of Elliott's record pole speed of 209.398 mph established May 2. But just eight caution laps – the lowest at Talladega since the 16 run in the 1983 Talladega 500 – assured the record-breaking speed.

Elliott ran laps consistently in the 202-205 mph range, most of which came after he doggedly made up lost ground following his sudden mechanical problem on lap 48 of the 188-lap race.

Going into the first turn, smoke erupted from the rear of Elliott's Thunderbird and the immediate diagnosis was that he had experienced a blown engine – something that happened to him in the 1982 season.

"I didn't know what it was," said Elliott, who picked up

Consistently turning laps at over 200 mph, Elliott came from two laps down to torch the field.

1985 Winston 500 Top Ten

Finish	Start	No.	Driver	Team/Owner	Laps	Money
1	1	9	Bill Elliott	Melling Racing	188	$60,500
2	4	7	Kyle Petty	Wood Brothers	188	34,905
3	2	28	Cale Yarborough	Ranier-Lundy	188	37,750
4	17	22	Bobby Allison	DiGard	187	23,075
5	15	15	Ricky Rudd	Bud Moore	187	21,025
6	32	88	Buddy Baker	Baker-Schiff Racing	185	20,245
7	3	44	Terry Labonte	Billy Hagan	185	20,100
8	18	71	Dave Marcis	Marcis Racing	185	12,575
9	7	8	Bobby Hillin, Jr.	Stavola Brothers	184	7,800
10	20	75	Lake Speed	RahMoc	183	11,215

Time of Race: 2 hours, 41 minutes, 4 seconds
Pole Winner: Bill Elliott – 209.398 mph
Average Speed: 186.288 mph
Cautions: 2 for 8 laps
Margin of Victory: 1.72 seconds
Attendance: 122,000

$60,500 for his victory. "I thought at first it was a broken transmission seal or gasket or something. Ernie (brother and crew chief) came on the radio and asked me, 'Is the engine blown?'

"I said the car was still running, and he told me to pit. We found it was a loose oil line. Before that, I nearly panicked. I had that feeling in my stomach which said it was time to take the car to the garage area and come back another day."

The pit stop for repairs took one minute, nine seconds, but to Elliott it was an eternity. He returned to the race just three seconds away from two laps in arrears to leader Kyle Petty in the Wood Brothers/ 7-Eleven Thunderbird.

"I honestly didn't think we could make it up," said Elliott. "I needed a caution and, of course, there weren't any until near the end when I didn't need 'em."

Elliott was able to gain ground on leaders Petty, Dale Earnhardt and Cale Yarborough because of his car's superior speed. But because of his lengthy unscheduled stop, he was out of the regular pit stop rotation. He pitted anywhere from eight to 10 laps behind the leaders.

As a result, he would regain his lost lap when the others pitted, only to lose it a handful of laps later.

But by virtue of the strength of his car, Elliott kept closing the distance under the green. He was running second to leader Yarborough following a pit stop on lap 122 for right-side tires. On lap 125, Elliott passed Yarborough to regain his lost lap for the final time.

On lap 145, Elliott shot by Yarborough's Ranier/Hardee's Thunderbird low in the third turn and began running laps in excess of 204 mph. Yarborough reassumed the lead after the day's first caution on lap 169. Elliott regained the No. 1 spot in the first turn and was never threatened, slowly but steadily pulling away by a half-second per lap.

"I knew how tough Cale was," said Elliott, who led four times for 60 laps. "So that's why I did my best to get away from him. It had been basically him and me all day and I felt if I caught him with the other cars I could get them all racing behind me and use that to get away from him."

Yarborough had problems of his own. With Elliott escaping at the end and eventually winning by at least 30 car lengths, the driver from Sardis, S.C., who has yet to win this year in his new Thunderbird, found himself in a scrap for second place with Petty.

Petty took the outside route through the fourth turn and ran alongside Yarborough as the two sped through the front dogleg toward the finish line. As the checkered flag fell, Petty crossed the line no more than a fender length ahead of Yarborough to earn second place. He tied the highest finish of his career as his other second-place finish came at Dover, Delaware, in 1982. His winnings of $34,905 were the highest of his career.

"I knew Kyle had run good all day," said Elliott. "But I didn't know if he would help or hurt Cale in the draft. Sometimes a good drafting car can help you or it can hurt you. I did figure he would be in the race for it in the end."

"I tried to catch Bill on the last restart, but I found out real quick I couldn't. Then came Kyle. I knew he was in the right place to make a pass, and I was trying to figure out a way to hold him off or pass him back in the trioval. I guess I just came up a little short," said Yarborough.

"Cale was behind us on the last restart and I thought, 'Uh-oh, he has me where he wants me,'" said Petty. "But then he blew by me chasing Bill. On the last lap he went low, and I had the momentum so I went on the high side, like Daddy (Richard) did at Daytona. I wanted to keep him pinched down in the corner and down the trioval to the flag so he wouldn't have a good run at me."

Only three cars finished on the lead lap, very unusual for Talladega, where long-train, multicar drafts and finishes have been the rule. Finishing fourth, one lap down, was Bobby Allison in the DiGard/Miller American Buick. He edged out fifth-place Ricky Rudd in the Moore/Motorcraft Thunderbird while Buddy Baker finished sixth, two laps down, in the Bull Frog/Liquid Wrench Oldsmobile. It was a very good day for Baker, who started 32nd.

Terry Labonte, defending Winston Cup champion, wound up seventh in the Hagan/Piedmont Airlines Chevrolet Monte Carlo while Dave Marcis was eighth in the AEL Rentals Monte Carlo. Bobby Hillin Jr. was ninth in the Trap Rock Industries Monte Carlo and Lake Speed rounded out the top 10 in the Rahmoc/Nationwise Pontiac.

Eighteen cars were running at the finish, with some of the notable dropouts being Darrell Waltrip and Neil Bonnett of the Johnson/Budweiser teams, Harry Gant in the Skoal Bandit Monte Carlo, Richard Petty in the Curb/STP Pontiac and Earnhardt in the Childress/Wrangler Monte Carlo, all victims of blown engines.

David Pearson retired with a malfunctioning carburetor, a broken transmission sidelined Joe Ruttman and Benny Parsons was forced out because of a wheel bearing.

"With what I had to do, it was a credit to my car and the team," said Elliott, whose four wins in the first five superspeedway races matches Pearson's accomplishment in 1976. "I felt that the engine was good, and if it held together, I would be able to hold my own after that long pit stop. But it was only after the others either dropped out or fell back and left Cale running by himself that I felt I could catch him.

"But I was never comfortable with it all. You are never really comfortable in a race car."

By Steve Waid

17

The Last Gas(p) Enough For Cale

Yarborough Wins Fast Winston 500

You want competitive racing? You like seeing cars swap the lead time and time again? That's what fans got at Talladega Superspeedway in a race run before the restrictor-plate era began. The Winston 500 featured a record 71 lead changes among 13 drivers – and those changes were only the ones counted at the start-finish line. The issue wasn't settled until the last lap. Cale Yarborough made the "slingshot" pass around Harry Gant and then, remarkably, held on to win despite running out of gas coming out of turn four. Yarborough did all he could to nurse the car to the checkered flag, and he did it successfully.

—Steve Waid

Like it said in the old coffee commercial, Cale Yarborough's Ranier/Hardee's Chevrolet Monte Carlo was "good to the last drop" in today's Winston 500 at Alabama International Motor Speedway.

With an empty gas tank and a sputtering engine, Yarborough managed to hold off Harry Gant's Skoal Bandit Monte Carlo and win the race by one car length. It was Yarborough's second victory of the season and the 80th of his career, which ties him for third place with Bobby Allison on NASCAR's all-time list. It also gave him the distinction of winning both races – the Daytona 500 and the Winston 500 – for which he had won both pole positions at over 200 mph.

But had Yarborough not done some quick thinking on the 188th and final lap, the laurel would have gone to Gant. After using the "slingshot" pass to get around Gant on the back straight of the 2.66-mile AIMS trioval, Yarborough felt the engine sputter as he roared out of the fourth turn and toward the checkered flag.

He managed to finish first by rocking the car, pumping the accelerator and using slower traffic.

"I ran out of gas in the fourth turn," said the 43-year-old Yarborough of Sardis, S.C. "I felt the engine sputter and I didn't have any idea I could make it to the finish line. But I rocked the car back and forth a bit and pumped it. That helped. We had stretched the gas mileage and knew it was going to be very, very close."

It was about as close as the competition. There were a NASCAR Winston Cup record 71 lead changes among 13 competitors in today's event, besting the old mark of 67 lead changes established for the 1978 Talladega 500, won by Lennie Pond. Because there were only four caution flags for 17 laps, the average speed of the race was 172.988 mph, a Winston 500 record.

Although the field was routinely stuck together in long, snake-like drafts of 20 or more cars throughout the day, as the waning laps came around, Gant, Buddy Baker in the Wood Brothers/Valvoline Ford Thunderbird and Benny Parsons in the

Even on his 80th trip, Cale Yarborough under-
stands how special victory lane is.

A record-setting 71st lead change sent Cale Yarborough to victory lane.

1984 Winston 500 Top Ten

Finish	Start	No.	Driver	Team/Owner	Laps	Money
1	1	28	Cale Yarborough	Ranier-Lundy	188	$42,300
2	11	33	Harry Gant	Mach 1 Racing	188	31,780
3	7	21	Buddy Baker	Wood Brothers	188	22,250
4	14	22	Bobby Allison	DiGard	188	31,250
5	4	55	Benny Parsons	Johnny Hayes	188	19,650
6	13	43	Richard Petty	Curb Motorsports	187	18,495
7	21	66	Phil Parsons	Johnny Hayes	187	11,000
8	23	75	Dave Marcis	RahMoc Racing	187	16,800
9	2	9	Bill Elliott	Melling Racing	187	14,600
10	19	47	Ron Bouchard	Race Hill Farm	186	11,525

Time of Race: 2 hours, 53 minutes, 27 seconds
Pole Winner: Cale Yarborough — 202.692 mph
Average Speed: 172.988 mph
Cautions: 4 for 17 laps
Margin of Victory: 2 car lengths
Attendance: 115,000

Hayes/Copenhagen Monte Carlo broke away and locked up in a three-car draft.

Baker and Parsons took command after making pit stops on lap 145. Gant then pitted on lap 152 and soon made it a three-car lead draft.

Yarborough would have made it a four-car draft, but he had problems when he pitted on lap 153. "I ran out of gas coming out of the second turn just before I made that stop," he explained. "So I had to coast into the pits, and that cost me about a quarter of a lap. So I was a quarter of a lap behind them when I came out."

Yarborough's crew chief, Waddell Wilson, figured that the Hardee's car had enough gas to turn 35 laps, which was exactly the number of circuits remaining at the time of the stop.

"But I had to run real hard to catch the leaders because I was so far behind and I knew that I was burning up fuel a bit faster than we wanted," said Yarborough, who won the second Winston 500 of his career today. "Even when I finally caught the leaders, I didn't pass. I just stayed in the draft, trying to conserve fuel as much as I could."

There was no such strategy available to Baker and Parsons, however. Because they pitted eight laps before Yarborough (and seven before Gant), they had no hope of finishing the race without stopping to take fuel. Both did on lap 177, leaving the chase to Gant and Yarborough.

When they pitted, Yarborough moved into second place and had Gant right where he wanted him – in the perfect position to make the quick pass so often used in the high-speed drafts created at Talladega and Daytona.

"But even on the white-flag (last) lap, I hadn't come up with an idea of where to pass Harry," said Yarborough. "I knew I was going to make my move either on the back straight or in turn four. When I came out of turn two I looked over the situation

and decided to pass on the back straight, going into the third turn."

Yarborough had spotted slower traffic ahead and figured he needed to lead in order to take advantage of it and keep Gant from using it against him.

Yarborough led Gant through a couple of slower cars going into the fourth turn, but coming out of it, his sputtering engine told him he was out of gas.

"I told him over the radio to shake the car and then to use the car in front of him to block Harry if he could," said Wilson. "Maybe by using the slower car he could mess Harry up a bit."

Yarborough responded by shooting to the inside of Trevor Boys' Monte Carlo through the track dogleg, leaving Gant no room to the inside and effectively cutting off a passing route.

"It was good split-second thinking by Cale," said Wilson.

"On the last lap I was trying to get as big a jump on Cale as I could," said Gant, who has now finished second 15 times in his Winston Cup career. "I saw some slower traffic ahead of me and I was trying to hold him off as best I could. But he got through,

and when we came into turns three and four, I saw Trevor Boys on the inside – and I saw Cale wiggle real bad. I know now that he was out of gas.

"But by that time, Boys went outside after Cale shot right down on his bumper. I knew it was all over then. I didn't have an outside or inside route to take. Cale was making the most of the race track."

There was an exciting battle for third place. That was taken by Baker, who was only inches ahead of Bobby Allison's DiGard/Miller High Life Monte Carlo, which, in turn, was only another few inches ahead of Parsons in a three-abreast finish.

Yarborough's victory was another in what he hopes will be at least four – make that "Big Four" – this year. "The 'Big Four' are the Daytona 500, the Winston 500, the World 600 (at Charlotte, N.C.), and the Southern 500 (at Darlington, S.C.)," said Yarborough. "It's one of my goals to win them for my car owner, Harry Ranier."

He's halfway there.

By Steve Waid

The field gets in line for what would be one of the greatest NASCAR races of all time.

DOZIER MOBLEY PHOTO

18

Bouchard Stuns 'Em At Talladega

First Win For Rookie Driver

Ron who? That's what fans asked after the conclusion of the Talladega 500. Ron was Ron Bouchard, a rookie who pulled off a monumental upset by making a three-wide move at the finish line to beat Darrell Waltrip and Terry Labonte. Bouchard became the first rookie to win a superspeedway race and became the 13th different driver to win a race in the 13-year-history of the Talladega 500. Bouchard might have been a rookie, but he made a veteran's move when he saw Waltrip and Labonte move to the high side as they came toward the checkered flag. He shot to the low side to beat Waltrip by a nose. Waltrip said he never saw Bouchard coming.

—Steve Waid

The mystique that surrounds the Talladega 500 at Alabama International Speedway continues for another year.

This Winston Cup race supplied a 13th different winner in its 13-year existence today after rookie driver Ron Bouchard, at the outset an unlikely candidate for victory, won a thrilling, last-lap duel with Darrell Waltrip and Terry Labonte.

Driving the Jack Beebe-owned Race Hill Farm Buick based in Connecticut, Bouchard, of Fitchburg, Mass., won his first Grand National race by a mere two feet over Waltrip's Junior Johnson/Mountain Dew Buick, which in turn nipped Labonte's Stratagraph Buick by another foot as the excited crowd of 75,000 stood and watched.

In continuing Talladega's remarkable streak of a different winner each year in this event, Bouchard also became the second rookie to win a Winston Cup event this year. It is the first time two rookies have won in a single season. Morgan Shepherd, the current Champions Spark Plug Rookie of the Year points leader, won the Virginia 500 at Martinsville Speedway in April.

Bouchard is the first rookie to win a superspeedway race.

"It's the greatest feeling in the world to win a Grand National race," said Bouchard, 32. "And tomorrow I'll probably feel the same way. I was fortunate at the end; I was in the right place at the right time."

That Bouchard's Buick – prepared under the direction of crew chief Bob Johnson – was in a position to win the race was no surprise after the green flag fell.

Bouchard was always in the lead lap and was one of 11 drivers that swapped the lead 36 times. On the final lap, he was running third, behind Waltrip and Labonte, when some strategy and a bit of good fortune paid off in victory.

"Coming off the fourth turn into the trioval, I was behind Waltrip and Terry, when Terry decided to pass Darrell on the outside," Bouchard explained. "When he moved up, Darrell

Terry Labonte (44) and Ron Bouchard (47) battled for much of the day.

DAVID CHOBAT PHOTO

moved up to get in front of him. When I saw that, I just shot down to the inside and got a push or something extra and moved up fast.

"I'm not sure Darrell saw me. I'm sure he knew I was around because I'd been running with him all day. But by the time he saw me, I was already three-quarters past him. I thought I had beaten him to the finish line by a foot or so, but I wasn't sure.

"I asked Bob on the radio as I went down the backstretch, but the radio wasn't working. Only when I looked up and saw my number in first place on the scoreboard was I sure I'd won the race."

Waltrip was trying to win his eighth race of the season, and he apparently thought Labonte was the man he had to beat.

"Terry and I got to racing each other and completely forgot about ol' Ron Bouchard," said Waltrip. "Where did he come from anyway? When we got three abreast going for the flag, I was doing all I could to hold off Terry, and then along sneaks Bouchard.

"If the start-finish line was up here where it ought to be you wouldn't see anything like this. Typical Talladega. Who knows what's going to happen in this race? Terry and I were side by side, and Bouchard beats me by six inches, and I beat Terry by about six inches. Bouchard went by me and Terry like we were tied to a tree somewhere."

Labonte stalked Waltrip for several laps, waiting for what he hoped would be the right moment to make the typical Talladega "slingshot" to the checkered flag.

"I guess this is what you'd call a tough break," said Labonte, still looking for his first win of the season." I thought I had Darrell right where I wanted him on the last lap. I was running right ahead of him going through the trioval, and then Bouchard sneaks under both of us at the flag."

Bay State resident Bouchard speaks with a heavy

Boston accent and has been a Modified driver for 16 years. He is a two-time champion at the speedways at Stafford Springs and Thompson, Conn., and a five-time champ at Seekonk, Mass.

He has competed in only 11 Grand National races, having taken the Beebe team ride in March after Harry Gant quit following the Atlanta 500.

With eight laps remaining, Bobby Allison, who appeared to have the strongest car in the field, dropped off the pace when a cylinder failed in his Hardee's Buick. Just four laps earlier, Gant's Skoal Bandit Pontiac also gave up the chase when his car began vibrating badly.

As a result, Gant finished fourth and Allison fifth. Lake Speed finished sixth in spite of a spin that brought out the final caution on lap 170. Kyle Petty was seventh in the STP Buick (his father, Richard, suffered engine failure after just 12 laps), and Jody Ridley took eighth in a Ford. Stan Barrett was ninth in a Skoal Pontiac, while Dave Marcis finished 10th in a Buick.

Cale Yarborough finished 28th after a wreck with Rick Watson on lap 83, the same lap that saw Dale Earnhardt retire with transmission troubles. Defending champion Neil Bonnett was out of the race after completing just 41 laps before ignition problems struck his Purolater Thunderbird.

James Hylton, running the race with STP sponsorship, did not fare as well. He finished 39th

Bouchard, a rookie, enjoys the spoils of his first trip to victory lane.
DAVID CHOBAT PHOTO

after suffering a broken drive shaft.

"We didn't have any problems," said Bouchard, who earned $38,805. "The car ran well right off the truck. We only made small changes. It was right on the money."

And at just the right moment at Alabama International Speedway today, so was Ron Bouchard. 🏁

By Steve Waid

117

19

Waltrip Nips Petty For Rebel Win

Photo Finish For Second

Darrell Waltrip was a brash upstart who had ruffled competitors' and fans' feathers with his self-confidence and candor. But he could drive a racecar. Richard Petty was NASCAR's now and forever King and widely admired by everyone. So when the kid and the King went at it at Darlington Raceway, it was a duel for the ages. The final 83 laps were a two-car battle that saw both drivers do things drivers weren't supposed to do at Darlington. Waltrip and Petty swapped the lead seven times over the closing laps. In the end, Waltrip nipped Petty for the victory in a dramatic photo finish. It was the biggest win in Waltrip's young career.

—**Steve Waid**

"I feel at my age and experience, I am the best race driver I could be," said Darrell Waltrip, the former controversial driver who now wears a "white hat."

Waltrip, 32, beat old pro Richard Petty in a heart-stopping, thrilling finish to the 23rd annual CRC Rebel 500 Sunday before 50,000 fans at Darlington Raceway.

It was Waltrip's second Rebel 500 victory in three years, and he called it his most satisfying win. Compared to victories at Talladega and Charlotte, he said, "They were nice, but they weren't at Darlington."

It was a photo finish before the largest crowd ever to see the Rebel race. Waltrip nipped Petty by two-tenths of a second, while Donnie Allison was only a hood behind Petty in third place. All three were driving Chevrolet Monte Carlos.

The final 83 of the 367 laps were a duel between Petty, who hasn't won here since 1967, and Waltrip, the young driver who took exception to most of what "King Richard" had to say.

They swapped the lead back and forth seven times over those 83 laps, and they raced side by side off and on all the while. There were several unofficial changes, like when Petty would pass Waltrip in the second turn, but lose the lead again in the third and fourth.

"We touched several times," Waltrip said, "but not on the last lap. After he'd hit me or I'd hit him, he would wave or I would wave. We knew the show was still going on. It was a clean battle. I never thought for once he would do anything to wreck me. It was tight, but fair and square."

It was Waltrip's second win of the season, 17th of his career and number eight on the Winston Cup circuit's superspeedways. He's 22nd on the all-time win list and 10th in superspeedway wins.

Waltrip averaged 121.721 mph in a race slowed six times for 53 laps. For the seventh time in eight races this year, the weather played a factor. Late in the race, rain hit the track, extending the final caution of the day for several minutes.

The Franklin, Tenn., resident led 10 times for 241 laps. Petty was next as the lap leader, setting the pace five times for 90 laps. They led all but 36 laps.

Waltrip regained the lead in the Winston Cup standings

Winning at Darlington for the second time in three years, Darrell Waltrip's excitement could not be contained.

DOZIER MOBLEY PHOTO

Six-time Rebel winner David Pearson was finished for the day when his left side wheels fell off leaving pit road after an abbreviated stop.

DOZIER MOBLEY PHOTO

1979 Rebel 500 Top Ten

Finish	Start	No.	Driver	Team/Owner	Laps	Money
1	2	88	Darrell Waltrip	DiGard	367	$23,400
2	6	43	Richard Petty	Petty Enterprises	367	16,100
3	1	1	Donnie Allison	Hoss Ellington	367	13,650
4	5	27	Benny Parsons	M.C. Anderson	365	5,700
5	7	28	Buddy Baker	Harry Ranier	365	8,500
6	9	11	Cale Yarborough	Junior Johnson	364	9,450
7	12	9	Bill Elliott	George Elliott	362	3,700
8	4	90	Ricky Rudd	Junie Donlavey	360	5,950
9	16	05	Dick Brooks	Nelson Malloch	360	3,150
10	20	72	Joe Millikan	L.G. DeWitt	358	7,250

Time of Race: 4 hours, 6 minutes, 59 seconds
Pole Winner: Donnie Allison – 154.797 mph
Average Speed: 121.721 mph
Cautions: 6 for 53 laps
Margin of Victory: Half car length
Attendance: 50,000

from Bobby Allison, who exited with engine failure on the 264th lap. Waltrip now has an 81-point lead over Allison in the point standings.

About two-thirds of the way into the race, Waltrip had a 12-second lead over Petty. Suddenly, Waltrip slowed coming off the second turn. He pitted and slipped to third place.

"Ricky Rudd hit the wall in the second turn and dropped some debris. I ran over it but couldn't tell what tire was flat. I had just lapped Donnie. He came back around me and indicated it was my right front. I took his word and changed right-side tires. That was the biggest single factor in the win," Waltrip said.

One problem or another eliminated most of the favorites from the chase for the checkered flag. Shortly after Waltrip's cut tire, David Pearson punctured a tire and made an unscheduled stop. He lost a lap.

Pearson, a six-time winner in this event, tried several times to get himself unlapped. He was in a good position to do it on the fifth caution, which came out after Neil Bonnett hit the first-turn wall. But Pearson

left the pits before new tires could be bolted on the left side, and the old wheels came off at the end of pit road. That finished him for the day.

"Darrell could fly on the straights. I was making it up in the turns. My car was handling real well in the turns, and I knew I had a shot at winning," said Petty.

"Then along came Donnie. We all had a chance to win. I wanted to win, but I didn't want to finish third. Donnie and I got a bit crowded coming off number four, but it didn't make any difference. Darrell had both of us beat at that time," Petty said of the last lap.

Waltrip took the lead in the first turn on the last lap, and Donnie Allison almost took both of them. "Once they got to jockeying on the last lap, I figured I had it made," said Waltrip.

"At the end I was running just as hard as I could," Donnie Allison said. "I wasn't thinking about anything else. It was a good clean race, and the fans got their money's worth. Three of us had a shot at it. That's the kind of competition we have on the circuit right now."

"It was a real tense race," said Petty. "About as tense as I can remember lately. It must have been a good show."

Benny Parsons and Buddy Baker made it a Chevy sweep of the first five positions in the 36-car field. They were fourth and fifth respectively, two laps behind.

Cale Yarborough, three laps down in the Junior Johnson Olds, was sixth. He never led a lap and ran out of gas three times. He also tangled with Pearson earlier in the race, but the latter was able to remain in the lead lap.

It was the most spectacular race ever held here. It was mostly ho-hum until the live TV cameras of ABC came on at 4:30 p.m. The action picked up, and the race wound up with a typical Darlington finish.

By Gene Granger

Trading the lead seven times in the closing laps, Petty and Waltrip put on quite a show.

DOZIER MOBLEY PHOTO

20

It's Labonte In A Cloud Of Smoke

Wild Finish To Wild Race

As usual, carnage marked yet another race at Bristol Motor Speedway, a fast, unforgiving half-miler. And as usual, Dale Earnhardt was right in the middle of it. Seems Terry Labonte was in the lead with just 12 laps remaining in the race. He looked to be a sure bet for victory. But on the last lap, Labonte became entangled in traffic, which allowed Earnhardt, the pursuer, to close. On the last lap, it happened. Earnhardt popped the rear end of Labonte's car and it went spinning out of control - right across the finish line. For all his efforts, Earnhardt only served to punt Labonte to victory. His car became one of the many severely damaged, but Labonte didn't care - he won.

—Steve Waid

Terry Labonte emerged as the winner in a wildly improbable finish to a wildly improbable Goody's 500.

In an exciting conclusion to a race marked by carnage, Labonte's Hendrick Motorsports Chevrolet crossed the finish line sideways, with the brakes squealing and smoking, then smashed into the frontstretch wall just 0.1-second ahead of Dale Earnhardt, the driver who provided much of the drama to the 500-lap race on the 0.533 mile, high-banked Bristol track. Earnhardt staged not one, but two thrilling charges from the rear of the field to the front to be in a position to challenge for the victory.

Even Labonte admitted he's never quite experienced a victory like this one.

"It was exciting at the end, wasn't it?" Labonte said from victory lane. "I thought I had enough laps left to hold off Earnhardt, but I came up on some lapped cars, and they didn't seem to think too much of getting out of the way.

"Then Dale ran into the back of me, but I stayed on the gas. I bounced off one of the lapped cars and into the wall. Funny thing, but I didn't even put a scratch on my car until the end."

Labonte led only the last 69 laps of the race marred by 15 caution periods – nearly all of which were caused by car-shredding accidents – for 106 laps. If any car escaped unscathed, no one saw it.

When the 15th and final caution ended on lap 400, Dale Jarrett was in the lead with Labonte in second place. On lap 432, Labonte charged to the inside of Jarrett in the second turn to take the lead he would hold until the wild conclusion.

Earnhardt moved into position to challenge by swarming his competition. After the final restart, he was not among the top 10. But by lap 473, he was in fifth place. Then, on lap 488, he overtook Jarrett for second.

With 12 laps remaining, Labonte's lead seemed safe. But on the last lap, he was caught by traffic, which allowed Earnhardt to close in on his rear bumper. Then, coming out of the fourth turn, Earnhardt tapped Labonte's rear…and the end was pure Hollywood.

"When I ran down Jarrett, I knew I was faster in the corners than he was, and he was a little loose," said Labonte, who won $66,940. "Then I saw Earnhardt get by him, and I knew he had fresher tires. Ours were pretty worn.

Battered and broken, but not beaten, Terry
Labonte's Monte Carlo made it to victory lane.

Early in the race, Earnhardt didn't need to tap Labonte to get ahead.

1995 Goody's 500 Top Ten

Finish	Start	No.	Driver	Team/Owner	Laps	Money
1	2	5	Terry Labonte	Hendrick Motorsports	500	$66,940
2	7	3	Dale Earnhardt	RCR Enterprises	500	66,890
3	16	28	Dale Jarrett	Robert Yates Racing	500	39,390
4	20	17	Darrell Waltrip	DarWal Inc.	500	32,780
5	1	6	Mark Martin	Roush Racing	500	41,775
6	4	24	Jeff Gordon	Hendrick Motorsports	500	27,865
7	19	4	Sterling Marlin	Morgan-McClure	500	26,140
8	27	90	Mike Wallace	Donlavey Racing	500	14,840
9	18	8	Jeff Burton	Stavola Brothers	500	22,515
10	10	12	Derrike Cope	Bobby Allison Mtspt.	499	20,565

Time of Race: 3 hours, 15 minutes, 3 seconds
Pole Winner: Mark Martin — 125.093 mph
Average Speed: 81.979 mph
Cautions: 15 for 106 laps
Margin of Victory: 0.10 second
Attendance: 50,000

"When I came up on the traffic at the end, I didn't know which car to follow – they were side by side. I caught them on the white flag and really caught 'em good coming for the checkered.

"I didn't think Earnhardt could catch me without traffic. As it turned out, I was watching him in the rearview mirror when I got boxed in the traffic, trying to figure out which way he would go. Then he tapped me. I stood on the gas, aimed the car at the finish line, and here I am.

"That's the first time I can remember a finish like that for me. I don't remember ever taking the checkered flag sideways."

Labonte said he wasn't mad at Earnhardt over the contact.

"I won the race, so I'm not mad," he said. "If he had won the race, I might be a little mad. But I don't think he intended to wreck us. We were both trying to win the race."

That the race was even run was a surprise to most, given that steady rain postponed the start by 90 minutes and threatened to delay it by at least a day. The rain sidelined the drivers several times. During one rain delay the fans entertained themselves by starting a wave, which gained momentum after crew members lined up on pit wall and participated.

Shortly afterwards, Labonte was the designated "rabbit" and took a lap at speed after which he reported the track surface was suitable for racing. At 9:09 p.m., the green flag flew.

The field quickly fell into single file; there was no passing as the drivers cautiously began to work in a racing groove.

But it didn't take long for things to heat up. On lap 31, Rusty Wallace was sent spinning out of the fourth turn and into the wall at the flagstand after his Ford received a tap in the rear from Earnhardt's Chevrolet. The two were running fourth and fifth, respectively.

Obviously irate over the incident that cost him a lap, Wallace sped around the track and drove menacingly alongside Earnhardt under the caution. Twice, Earnhardt had to swerve to the left to avoid what he thought was imminent contact.

Before the race restarted on lap 38, NASCAR ordered Earnhardt to the rear of the field as punishment for his involvement in the accident.

On lap 51, the second caution began after Brett Bodine's Ford smacked the fourth-turn wall. Misfortune continued to plague Bodine. On lap 61, he took a hit from Bobby Hamilton's Pontiac and spun into the first-turn wall. NASCAR promptly black-flagged Hamilton to the "penalty box" for five laps. Bodine, meanwhile, spent 42 laps in the pits for repairs.

The race restarted on lap 66 with Jeremy Mayfield still in the lead, but on lap 74, rain began to fall, and the race was yellow-flagged for the fourth time. Seventeen laps later, the race restarted again.

The mayhem continued. The seventh caution was a result of a multicar accident on lap 234, triggered after Mayfield was sent spinning down the backstretch.

The race had hardly restarted on lap 245 when the eighth caution kicked in after Spencer made contact with Greg Sacks and sent him into the third-turn wall. Again, a multicar accident was the result.

Earnhardt retook the lead on lap 308 and held it through a series of pit stops after the 10th caution period, caused when Ricky Craven spun into the fourth-turn wall.

But on lap 329, Jarrett grabbed the lead out of the fourth turn. At the same time, Earnhardt was sent back to third place as he was sent high in turn one after contact with Derrike Cope, who inherited second place.

Jarrett held the lead through cautions 11, 12, 13, 14 and 15 while Earnhardt's fortunes waned. He

was forced to pit twice during the 13th caution, which began on lap 363, after his car began smoking due to a cracked oil cooler, the result of the contact with Cope.

Labonte ended Jarrett's dominance – the Ford driver led 99 laps – on lap 432, and then Earnhardt helped set up the finish when he passed Jarrett with 12 laps to go.

"We felt like the second half of the season would be better for us than the first," said Labonte, who has won at Richmond and Pocono this year and gave Hendrick Motorsports its eighth victory of the season. "We had a great car all night long and that's because of the guys on the team. They make it easier for me as good as all these cars are today.

"Hopefully, this will be the start of a few more races we'll win."

But it is safe to say Labonte would rather not win them in the fashion he did in the Goody's 500.

By Steve Waid

After taking the checkered flag sideways, Labonte enjoys the peace and quiet of victory lane.

'Lucky' Gant Snares Fourth Straight

Stands At Threshold Of Setting Modern-Era Record

Harry Gant came to Martinsville Speedway on a roll. He had won three consecutive races and was the hottest driver in NASCAR. At Martinsville, he could make it four in a row. But things didn't go well. With 123 laps to go, Rusty Wallace got the nose of his car underneath Gant, they touched and Gant spun in front of the field. Gant's car got tagged a couple more times, and everyone figured it was the end of the day for the 51-year-old. Nope. After numerous pit stops under caution, Gant came roaring back. He took the lead with 47 laps to go and never looked back. Four in a row. No wonder he was called "Mr. September."

—Steve Waid

For Harry Gant, his fourth straight NASCAR Winston Cup victory wasn't his easiest, but it may have been his most satisfying.

Gant survived two incidents in the Goody's 500's later stages and nursed his ailing Oldsmobile to his third win at the 0.526-mile track and his fifth this season, making him the series' leader. The win makes him only the fourth driver to be victorious in four straight Winston Cup events in NASCAR's modern era, which began in 1971 when the season was reduced to about 30 annual races. Cale Yarborough accomplished the feat in 1976, Darrell Waltrip in 1981 and Dale Earnhardt in 1987.

Even though the victory was Gant's fourth straight Winston Cup win, it was his sixth overall in NASCAR competition as he also has won two Busch Series races this month.

"I'm not getting any better (with age), I think we're just getting luckier," said the 51-year-old Gant, who earned his first Winston Cup victory at Martinsville in the spring of 1982, also

with right-front end damage on his car.

"We were very lucky to come back today and win the race. We were lucky at Richmond; we've been lucky the last five races. We've had a super car, and the team has worked well.

"This one was the hardest (of the four to win). I had to pass more cars today than I have in the others."

Gant's "luck" allowed him to come back from an incident with Rusty Wallace that left his car with a mangled front end. The accident occurred on the second lap after the restart following the 13th caution flag, which ended on lap 375 of the 500-lap race.

On lap 377, Wallace stuck the nose of his Pontiac underneath Gant's Oldsmobile as they entered turn three. Wallace tagged Gant, who had led for 111 laps, and the veteran driver spun in front of the field. Morgan Shepherd's Ford caught the front end of Gant, and Wallace was hit by Derrike Cope. Dale Earnhardt shot out of the pack unscathed to take the lead, and Ricky Rudd scrambled to beat Earnhardt back to the

Racing to the checkered flag, Gant—in his beat up
Olds—held off a hard-charging Brett Bodine.
DAVID CHOBAT PHOTO

start-finish line to regain his lost lap.

"Rusty got a little overanxious and ran into me going into the corner," said Gant, who won $64,000 for first place.

"I didn't think about him diving on me and going into the corner. It was just racing.

"I guess he thought he could make it, but there was no way he was going to. I'm sure he hated it and didn't mean to do it. I couldn't believe the two potential winners were going to put each other out. That's what I was more aggravated about."

Following the accident Gant made several pit stops in a row – all under the caution – to have the damage repaired as well as could be expected under the circumstances. A total team effort paid off, as Gant beat the pace car to the exit of pit row every time.

"It bent our front wheel out a whole lot, and that really affected the car going into the corner," Gant noted. "I couldn't go in as good as I could before. I had to go a little slower. But it came out just as good. It definitely had a lot of push in the car.

"We had a lot of stuff rubbing the tires. We had a lot of stuff knocked loose that we had to get off the car. The main thing was they couldn't do anything in the time we had as far as resetting the front end. We just had to leave it like it was," he said.

"We had an oil cooler that was almost jammed into a wheel, and that was a big concern, too. We also had a brake duct knocked loose, and to get them off is what took so much time. We couldn't go out dragging them or they would have black-flagged us."

When the race restarted on lap 383, Gant was 12th.

"I was upset, but it was hurting my driving. I ran around 10 laps mad as a bull," Gant admitted. "Rusty was behind me, and I wanted him in front.

"I caught myself driving too deep into the corners. I backed off and took my time. I figured if I finished fifth or sixth that would be a good day. Then by taking it easy, running off the corners smooth I was able to catch up much quicker than when I was hot."

On lap 425, he passed Jimmy Hensley for fifth. Sixteen laps later, Gant took Ernie Irvan on the outside in turn one for second and soon challenged Brett Bodine for the lead.

On lap 448, Gant passed Bodine on the inside as they entered turn three, but Bodine wasn't ready to relinquish the top spot. When the two drove into turn one, Bodine took the inside line, and the right front of his Buick caught the left rear of Gant's Oldsmobile. Gant slid sideways, but he quickly regained control and five laps later he retook the lead for good on lap 454.

"He tapped me in the back end after I passed him, then he dropped in on me down here (turn two)," said Gant, who led five times for 226 laps, including the final 47. "I knew I was going to beat him all day, and he wasn't going to beat me at the end. So, I didn't worry too much about it.

"I thought I'd get him back after a while and not even touch you. I think a lot of times that makes a driver feel worse than to boot them. I think it makes them feel like they're not as good as a driver as they think they are.

"It just takes a little thinking, but a lot of drivers, if they don't think, they're not going to win any races."

Gant experienced no more problems the rest of the way and finished one second ahead of Bodine.

Gant used the same car and same engine he'd driven in his other three wins.

"We practice as little as we can to keep miles off the engine and off the drivetrain," said Gant, who noted the only time he tests during the season is at Daytona in preparation for the season opener.

"I set the car up one time for that particular way we want to race. When I get the feel I want in that particular line I'm going to run, we stop work on the car immediately."

Gant is attempting to avoid the hoopla surrounding his success this month, which has resulted in him being nicknamed "Mr. September," by staying away from his Taylorsville, N.C., home, which has an unlisted number.

"Things aren't too bad if I leave the house at 5 (a.m.) and don't come back until 9 that night," said Gant, who admitted he would like to be the series' top winner for a single season. "That's what I've been doing, avoiding a lot of people. I've just got things I want to do and forget about it.

"I just want to go on to my next race. So that's what I'm trying to do."

By Deb Williams

1991 Goody's 500 Top Ten

Finish	Start	No.	Driver	Team/Owner	Laps	Money
1	12	33	Harry Gant	Leo Jackson	500	$64,000
2	2	26	Brett Bodine	King Motorsports	500	36,625
3	5	3	Dale Earnhardt	RCR Enterprises	500	30,350
4	13	4	Ernie Irvan	Morgan-McClure	500	19,300
5	1	6	Mark Martin	Roush Racing	500	24,575
6	26	94	Terry Labonte	Billy Hagan	500	12,900
7	7	2	Rusty Wallace	Roger Penske	500	11,500
8	4	5	Ricky Rudd	Hendrick Motorsports	500	15,300
9	9	25	Ken Schrader	Hendrick Motorsports	500	10,700
10	18	24	Jimmy Hensley	Team III	499	12,135

Time of Race: 3 hours, 31 minutes, 42 seconds
Pole Winner: Mark Martin – 93.171 mph
Average Speed: 74.535 mph
Cautions: 15 for 81 laps
Margin of Victory: 1 second
Attendance: 46,000

22

Wild Finish Gives Kyle Petty No. 1

Heckuva Wreck Makes Petty A Winner

Kyle Petty was as surprised as anyone. He figured the best he was going to finish at Richmond Fairgrounds Raceway was third. Ahead of him, Dale Earnhardt and Darrell Waltrip were battling relentlessly. But something happened. On the last lap, Earnhardt, who had lost the lead to Waltrip, clipped Waltrip's car as the two headed into the third turn. Both drivers went into a wild spin that opened the door for Petty. No need to ask him what he did — he sped past the damaged cars and took the checkered flag for his first career NASCAR victory. He left Richmond a happy man. The same could not be said for either Earnhardt or Waltrip.

—Steve Waid

The Miller High Life 400 NASCAR Winston Cup race at Richmond Fairgrounds Raceway ended just like it began – with a stupendous multicar crash on lap 398 that took out two cars, either of which could have catapulted their drivers to victory. It paved the way for dark horse Kyle Petty's first NASCAR Winston Cup career win.

After the smoke had cleared and the carnage had been swept away, the 25,000 spectators who attended the 400-lap event on the 0.542-mile short track watched Petty, 25, of New London, N.C., drive his Wood Brothers/7-Eleven Ford Thunderbird into victory lane. It was the third-generation driver's initial win in 170 Winston Cup starts and the first for the famed Wood Brothers since Buddy Baker won the 1983 Firecracker 400 at Daytona Beach, Fla.

There were nine yellow-flag periods for 63 laps, but the one that led to Petty's win occurred with only two laps left in the race. Dale Earnhardt, in the Childress/Wrangler Chevrolet

Monte Carlo SS, had taken the lead from Joe Ruttman's Bernstein/Quaker State Buick LeSabre at the tail end of lap 343 and proceeded to pull away.

Ten laps before, Darrell Waltrip, driving the Johnson/Budweiser Chevrolet (who at one time was a lap down), edged past Petty and the Hendrick/Levi Garrett Chevrolet of Geoff Bodine into third. On the 348th circuit, Waltrip, a six-time winner at Richmond, blew past Ruttman on the front straightaway into second place and began his pursuit of Earnhardt.

Much as he did last fall when he ran down Terry Labonte to win the Wrangler SanforSet 400, Waltrip began to pressure Earnhardt relentlessly. He pulled closer and closer to the Wrangler car, and heading down the backstretch into the third corner, he just barely cleared Earnhardt's car.

Then in a split second, Earnhardt appeared to clip Waltrip's right-rear quarter panel, and both automobiles went into a wild spin. While Earnhardt managed to limp around to the front of the speedway and finish third, Waltrip's mangled

Petty celebrates his good fortune and big pay day.

1986 Miller High Life 400 Top Ten

Finish	Start	No.	Driver	Team/Owner	Laps	Money
1	12	7	Kyle Petty	Wood Brothers	400	$37,880
2	17	26	Joe Ruttman	King Motorsports	400	16,215
3	10	3	Dale Earnhardt	RCR Motorsports	400	19,310
4	23	22	Bobby Allison	Stavola Brothers	399	6,275
5	3	11	Darrell Waltrip	Junior Johnson	398	14,298
6	4	8	Bobby Hillin, Jr.	Stavola Brothers	398	7,240
7	19	12	Neil Bonnett	Junior Johnson	398	10,055
8	1	5	Geoff Bodine	Hendrick Motorsports	397	8,435
9	24	71	Dave Marcis	Marcis Racing	397	5,890
10	6	27	Rusty Wallace	Blue Max Racing	397	6,530

Time of Race: 3 hours, 2 minutes, 54 seconds
Pole Winner: Geoff Bodine — based on points — no time trials
Average Speed: 71.078 mph
Cautions: 8 for 63 laps
Margin of Victory: Under Caution
Attendance: 25,000

racer came to rest against the rear wall.

The mess also involved Bodine and Ruttman, who were clipped by Trevor Boys' U.S. Racing Chevrolet. Ruttman went into a wild slide into the muddy infield grass but managed to finish second. Earnhardt claimed third. Bobby Allison got through the melee to finish fourth, a lap down in the Stavola/Miller American Buick, and Waltrip took fifth, two laps off the pace.

"Our car didn't drive as good as it should have. It pushed pretty good all day long and was a fourth- or fifth-place car," said Petty. "We were fortunate enough to win the race.

"When I started off in the corner, I could see Bodine, but I couldn't see Waltrip or Earnhardt. I saw Bodine up against the wall, (and) really, there were fenders, bumpers and trash everywhere. I was just trying to weed my way through it.

"The first time by the wreck, I didn't see Ruttman, and I thought he won the race," added Petty. "You've got to be realistic. You come in with a fourth- or fifth-place car, and it (victory) means a lot.

"Things worked out for us real well."

While Petty was celebrating in victory lane and later chatting in the infield pressroom, Waltrip stood by his destroyed Chevrolet, quietly steaming. At first, he avoided talking to anyone but his crew, but later made a few comments concerning the fracas.

"I haven't ever had a run-in with Earnhardt before," he said. "Everyone else has, and he's not choosy.

"We got down on the backstretch and he turned left into me. I want to win as much as anybody else, but I've never tried to hurt anyone.

"I was a lap down most of the day and finally got it back," added Waltrip. "I raced him a couple of times today, but this is the all-time best. I've never had anything like this happen."

Ruttman, winless in 125 races dating back to 1977, was somewhat despondent over today's outcome. He referred to this event in 1983, when driving for the now-defunct Benfield/Levi Garrett team. He led 161 laps but finished seventh because a minor part malfunctioned in his car.

"Really, in my heart, I said, 'Here's a chance to win the race,'" he said. "I lost one here because of a fluke, and I thought I was going to make up for it.

"There was no question that Darrell and Dale were stronger than me and would pass me, but I thought I had myself in a position to avoid anything in front of me."

Although bumping and banging are an integral part of short-track racing, today's "frammin' and bammin'" was frequent and excessive. Petty's Ford was one of the few cars to show little or no abuse; however, only nine of the 31 starters failed to take the checkered flag.

The first caution came just nine laps into the event when Doug Hevron and Boys slid into the turn-four guardrail. The race resumed on lap 14 but was immediately slowed again when Lake Speed's Rahmoc/Nationwise Pontiac Grand Prix 2+2 plowed into the railing in turn two.

It was full speed ahead on lap 18, but on that lap Ron Bouchard's Curb/Valvoline Pontiac sprayed mud onto the track in turn three. He clipped Waltrip, and before it was over 11 other cars were involved in the event's second-biggest calamity.

Subsequent cautions continued to drop the average speed of the event.

No. 1 starter Bodine led the first 59 laps, and Dave Marcis, in the Helen Rae Special Chevrolet, went to the front for the next 12. Other lap leaders included Jimmy Means, Wallace, Earnhardt, Petty, Waltrip and Ruttman.

Earnhardt was clearly one of two dominant figures today (Waltrip was the other) and led four times for 299 laps. Petty led twice for four laps, including the all-important last three.

"When we got involved in the first wreck (the multicar, third-caution pileup), we knocked the front end out a little bit," said Petty. "But the win builds your confidence, and with 27 races to go you need all the confidence you can get.

"Eddie (Wood) was telling me on the radio that they (Waltrip and Earnhardt) were going for it. I never expected to win.

"I figured if they got together and ran slow enough, Ruttman and the (No.) 5 (Bodine) car would catch up," he said. "They were unfortunate, and we were fortunate. That's all it was."

It took Petty three hours, two minutes and 54 seconds to complete the race at an average speed of 71.087 mph. There were 11 lead changes among eight drivers and Petty won $37,880.

By Gary McCredie

Dale Earnhardt slides by Lake Speed's spinning Pontiac early in this wreck-prone race.

DAVID CHOBAT PHOTO

Darlington Raceway
Darlington, South Carolina
August 30, 1997

23

Feeling Like A Million Bucks

Gordon Claims Bonus, Point Lead With Darlington Victory

When Jeff Gordon came to Darlington Raceway, he had already accomplished more in a handful of years than anyone could have imagined. He was about to accomplish something else. But it wasn't easy. Yes, he was leading on the last lap. But Jeff Burton was charging – hard. He caught his rival and did everything he could – even deliver a hard bump on the frontstretch – to get around him. But to no avail. Gordon won his third straight Southern 500 and became the first driver to win The Winston Million since Bill Elliott did it in 1985. Gordon wasn't done, however. He went on to win the 1997 championship, his second in just three years.

—Steve Waid

Add another chapter to what has become a remarkable tale: that of Jeff Gordon's Winston Cup career.

Under improbable circumstances, Gordon, a 26-year-old who has accomplished more in five years than most stock car drivers do in a lifetime, overcame an ill-handling car, an encounter with the second-turn wall and the determination of Jeff Burton to win the Mountain Dew Southern 500 and $1 million from The Winston Million bonus program.

Gordon thus becomes only the second driver in Winston Cup history to win the $1 million bonus. Bill Elliott, enjoying a season that propelled him to immense popularity, won the bonus the first year it was offered in 1985.

Gordon might have been handed an oversized check for $1 million in victory lane after the Mountain Dew Southern 500, but make no mistake about it – he wasn't given anything. He earned it.

In one of the most exciting finishes in recent memory, Gordon edged a charging Jeff Burton by 0.144 second at the checkered flag to do something no other driver has ever done – win the Mountain Dew Southern 500 for the third straight time.

"This is just unbelievable," said an elated Gordon. "I never thought anyone would win the $1 million again, let alone three straight Southern 500's.

"This team won this race today. I might have had something to do with the last couple of laps, but it was the team today. They were awesome. They were taking spring rubbers out, then I was asking them to put them back in, and the thing of it was, they did it all without losing time.

"We earned it today."

Gordon, in a Chevrolet, had to win a last-lap duel with Burton, in a Ford, to claim the loot. And what a battle it was.

It was set up as Burton charged from seventh place to third to challenge second-place Dale Jarrett, who had been Gordon's

Jeff Gordon has a million reasons to smile.
DAVID CHOBAT PHOTO

Unable to stay out front the entire day, Gordon was forced to battle for every inch in winning his third straight Southern 500.

1997 Southern 500 Top Ten

Finish	Start	No.	Driver	Team/Owner	Laps	Money
1	7	24	Jeff Gordon	Hendrick Motorsports	367	$1,131,330
2	16	99	Jeff Burton	Roush Racing	367	57,280
3	3	88	Dale Jarrett	Robert Yates Racing	367	47,505
4	2	94	Bill Elliott	Bill Elliott Racing	367	49,965
5	21	10	Ricky Rudd	Rudd Perf. Mtspt.	367	39,345
6	17	5	Terry Labonte	Hendrick Motorsports	367	41,315
7	1	18	Bobby Labonte	Joe Gibbs Racing	367	42,240
8	4	6	Mark Martin	Roush Racing	367	35,550
9	14	21	Michael Waltrip	Wood Brothers	367	29,020
10	5	33	Ken Schrader	Andy Petree Racing	366	23,280

Time of Race: 4 hours, 8 minutes, 17 seconds
Pole Winner: Bobby Labonte – 170.661 mph
Average Speed: 121.149 mph
Cautions: 11 for 67 laps
Margin of Victory: 0.144 second
Attendance: 75,000

nemesis for most of the race's concluding laps.

Burton passed Jarrett on lap 364, and one lap later, he was on Gordon's tail. As they sped out of the fourth turn to take the white flag, the drama unfolded.

Burton, after gaining a rush of momentum off the fourth turn, squeezed to Gordon's inside.

The two bumped and rubbed sheet metal, courting disaster. But it was Gordon who nudged his way ahead, taking the outside line into the first turn. From there, Burton could not mount a second charge to the checkered flag.

"Out of the turn I had slid up, and I saw him coming," Gordon said. "So I moved down, and he plowed right into my rear end. It almost picked up the rear wheels. I was lucky I didn't spin out right there.

"Jeff slid sideways and got on the apron. Here, there's all that sand and debris he got on his tires. We banged into each other as we headed into the first turn, but then he had to let up because he was on ice. We talk about tire buildup, tire buildup. If he hadn't had it and he had waited until the last lap, he probably would have gotten me.

"For the final 30 laps I got all I could out of the car."

While Gordon, who started seventh, appeared to be a contender for most of the race, he said his Chevrolet was at best a fourth- or fifth-place car without adjustments. And for a while it appeared his chances for victory and the loot appeared dim.

After the race was about two-thirds completed, Gordon found himself battling handling problems.

On lap 307, Gordon nearly took himself out of the race. He scraped the wall coming out of turn two, and although he kept his lead over Jarrett, there was concern he had damaged his car.

"It just shocked me," Gordon said. "My car was running great through turn two. That's where I had been able to get away from Dale a little bit. I went in

there, accelerated, and the next thing I knew, bam! I hit the wall. If you lose focus for just a split second it will get you."

With 50 laps to go, Gordon's lead was 0.22 second, or about three car lengths. With 40 laps to go, Gordon, Jarrett, and Burton were locked in a three-car duel, each no more than two car lengths apart from each other.

Then, on lap 333, Ward Burton's Pontiac spun out of the second turn, directly in front of the trio of leaders. All of them avoided disaster and pitted under the 11th caution period of the race.

"That got pretty exciting," Gordon said. "I saw it happen out of the corner of my eye. I tried to figure out which way to go, and my spotter was trying to tell me when he saw the smoke. He said go low, and I went and got clear."

Again, Gordon was out of the pits first with Jarrett second. Burton fell to seventh after his crew had to replace lug nuts that had fallen off a left side wheel on his Ford.

When the race went back under the green on lap 339, Gordon was first, Jarrett second, Terry Labonte third, Ricky Rudd fourth and Mark Martin fifth.

Jarrett knew he had his last opportunity to snatch victory away from Gordon.

It evolved into a tense, dramatic finish.

Jarrett doggedly pursued Gordon, and with 10 laps to go, the two were nose to tail – and Burton was closing. Two laps later, Burton was on Jarrett's rear bumper, and it was a three-car duel again.

On lap 364, Burton swung low alongside Jarrett in the first turn and made the pass, which allowed Gordon to pad his lead slightly. But with two laps to go, his margin disappeared. Burton closed on Gordon's rear bumper and set up the drama on the last lap.

Even the guys from Winston were excited to part with $1M.

DAVID CHOBAT PHOTO

"Coming down to take the white flag, there was nothing I could do," Gordon said. "I had the wheel cranked as hard as I could; I was sliding to the wall. As I came off (turn) four, I moved down because he had a run going. As I moved down, that's when he plowed into the back of me and almost lifted the wheels.

"I can't imagine it getting more exciting than it was. I'm sure he's not happy because I ran him real hard. When it came down to the last lap, and I've said this all week, if I have a shot, or am in the lead, watch out because there's a guy going for a million bucks and three Southern 500's in a row."

"Gordon was going for the $1 million, and when I got under him, he cut down on me," Burton said. "If I had cut back down on him, I might have wrecked him. I'm not saying, though, that I might not have done the same thing. If I was going for the $1 million, I might have done the same thing."

Gordon's victory drove his career earnings to $13,668,532 and puts him sixth on NASCAR's all-time list. No other driver has earned more than $13 million as quickly as Gordon.

Just add that to the lengthy list of impressive achievements Gordon has compiled in a very, very short time. 🏁

By Steve Waid

2001 Pepsi 400

Morning Glory

Earnhardt Jr.'s win helps ease pain of February tragedy

In the first race at Daytona International Speedway since the tragic Daytona 500 in which Dale Earnhardt lost his life, his son, Dale Jr., had become the favorite of the fans. His name was Earnhardt, wasn't it? But would he fulfill his father's legacy? While the question is still unanswered, Dale Jr. went a long way toward providing the answer. With a stellar performance, he won the Pepsi 400. Emotions poured out as people realized the son had won on the track that had claimed his father just a few months earlier. Rest assured that fact was not lost on Dale Jr.

—Steve Waid

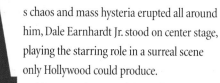s chaos and mass hysteria erupted all around him, Dale Earnhardt Jr. stood on center stage, playing the starring role in a surreal scene only Hollywood could produce.

Now one of America's most famous sons, he stood proudly in victory lane at Daytona International Speedway while fireworks lit up the night sky.

As sparks from the spectacular display rained down like confetti, a spotlight suddenly materialized in the midst of the vanishing smoke. It appeared to be a sign, a prophetic symbol from above.

It shone like the Bat signal lighting up Gotham City after Batman's latest triumph over evil. But this was no comic book/cartoon caricature. It was the white numeral 3, NASCAR's newest trademark and the symbol of its own superhero.

Ironically, the bright light represented both the legend of the great Dale Earnhardt and the symbolism of his death at the very track that now honored him.

The eerie sight was planned and orchestrated as yet another tribute to the seven-time champion, who was killed Feb. 18 on the final lap of the Daytona 500.

Yet of all the hokey memorials NASCAR fans have enjoyed, and endured, in the five months since Earnhardt's death (the flowerbeds in the shape of a 3, the weekly three-finger salute), this was by far the most bizarre.

Fittingly, it was set to appear at the conclusion of the Pepsi 400, Daytona's first race since the tragic event. What NASCAR and speedway officials couldn't plan was the appearance of Earnhardt Jr. in victory lane while his father's famous numeral filled the sky as bright as the moon.

No one this side of Hollywood could have written such a script. Not even NASCAR, the butt of frequent jokes about its mythical "fix," could have drummed this one up.

Even Earnhardt Jr., who as a child dreamed of such dramatic scenarios, couldn't fathom fate delivering such a feel-good chapter to a tragedy.

"As far as things being meant to happen, I always felt like that when I was a little kid ... but I was always let down," he said after his fairy-tale conquest. "I've been in situations like this before, where I was like, 'It would be cool if I won this or it would be cool if this happened or that happened' ... but things like that never happened."

Winning the first race back at Daytona since his father's death, Dale Earnhardt Jr. gave everyone something to celebrate.

NS ARCHIVE PHOTO

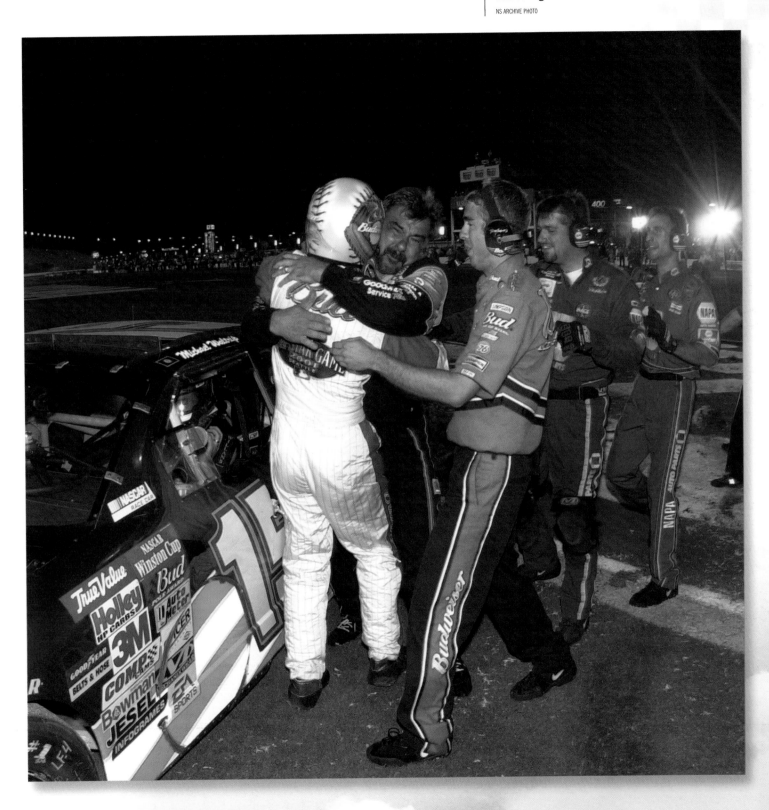

Dale Jr. passes Mike Skinner (31) on the inside and begins his dash to the front.

Some scenarios are just too perfect to have been dreamed up by some cheesy script writer. Who, for instance, would have believed that:

• Junior would win the first race at Daytona since his father's death there in February?

• Or that Dale Earnhardt Inc. would sweep the top two spots at Daytona again, just as it did the day Earnhardt died?

• Or that teammate Michael Waltrip would push Earnhardt Jr. across the finish line, just as Junior did for him in the infamous Daytona 500?

• Or that Waltrip would spend the final laps blocking for his teammate, just as Earnhardt Sr. was doing when his fatal crash occurred?

• Or that Junior would put the finishing touches on his greatest victory by spinning donuts in the trioval grass, just as his father did when he finally conquered the Daytona 500, his last win at the sacred track?

But in sports, as in movies, some things just seem destined to happen, and a victory by Junior seemed to be in the stars as the bereaved NASCAR community made the dreaded return to Daytona Beach.

The signs were everywhere: a full moon that loomed large over the city for three days before the Pepsi 400, a forbearer of something strange and mystical; the dark sky that descended on the speedway two days prior to the event, dumping rain on the track and sending columnists scurrying to their computers, pounding out the symbolism of the ominous black clouds; and the date of the race, 11 years to the day since Earnhardt Sr. won his first Pepsi 400 on July 7, 1990.

This one had a movie-like feel from the beginning, a supernatural plot that conjured up images of "Field Of Dreams" or "The Legend Of Bagger Vance."

Before he even set foot on the Daytona grounds, almost everyone seemed to believe that Earnhardt Jr. would win, just as they seemed to know that his father would finally win the 1998 Daytona 500 on his 20th try.

"There is no doubt he was the favorite before he got here this weekend," Winston Cup champion Bobby Labonte said. "He was the sentimental favorite, of course."

Even Junior seemed to know something special was going to happen. He was so relaxed that he told reporters he was actually looking forward to returning to Daytona, where he planned to relax and party on the beach with his friends. Following the race, Junior, Waltrip and friends gathered in the competitor's motorhome compound to listen to Edwin McCain strum his guitar.

Earlier, Earnhardt Jr. threw his own party on the track and it turned out to be the feel-good story of the year for the beleaguered sport, topping teammate Steve Park's win at Rockingham the week after Earnhardt's death and the stunning victory two weeks later by Kevin Harvick, the baby-faced rookie who replaced Earnhardt at Richard Childress Racing.

"I never would have imagined this happening," Earnhardt Jr. said. "I never would have imagined coming here and winning this race."

But everyone else did.

"It's hard to imagine anybody that you would want to win here any more than Little Earnhardt," Jeff Burton said. "This sport lost a hero. A lot of people lost a hero, but he lost a hero and his dad."

"That's perfect," said Rusty Wallace, who rode the bumper of Earnhardt Jr.'s fast car for about 30 laps. "I can't think of a better script than to come back to the track that took his father away from him. To be able to honor him with the victory is pretty cool."

Even those saddled with a bitter defeat realized the magnitude of Junior's triumph. For the second time in two years, Johnny Benson was leading at Daytona with only a few laps remaining, only to lose the lead and wind up 13th.

"But it's OK," Benson said. "It was good that Junior won. I'm glad that he won."

So was nearly everyone else. When Junior took the checkered flag, it sparked the type of celebration NASCAR has not enjoyed since his father won the Daytona 500. As the crews from DEI and RCR sprinted to the frontstretch grass, a crowd of more than 100,000 erupted with a deafening roar, prompting Junior and Waltrip to climb onto the roof of their stopped cars and share their joy, just as they had shared their grief.

For many fans, the win was not just a popular victory, but a bit of solace for the legion of Earnhardt supporters still mourning his death.

"All year long people have been telling me they have been pulling for me and people have been pushing for us to do well," Junior said. "You start feeling a little pressure, like we want to win for these people who are real dedicated to us and a lot of people who have become fans just recently. You want to win for them and give them reasons to pull for you. This was a good feeling. That's why I pulled down on the front straightaway and jumped out. That was for the fans and for nobody else."

The moment brought back memories of his first

Unforgettable.
NS ARCHIVE PHOTO

Winston Cup victory last year at Texas, when his father sprinted to victory lane, where Junior leaped into his arms. Or at Charlotte last May, when Junior turned his ear to the crowd as it chanted the Earnhardt name, his proud father passing the torch to his son.

Only this time, his father wasn't there, a cold, hard fact that needed no reminder, but that the eerie spotlight hammered home. That Junior was able to contain his emotions and muster the courage to even race at the track that claimed his father's life was an accomplishment in itself.

But as he has shown since the accident, he is mature beyond his 26 years, handling the devastating loss and the resulting media publicity with uncanny maturity.

"He did everything he could to steer away from that," fellow driver Mark Martin said. "He said he likes coming to Daytona and he was looking forward to it. He didn't start crying and say, 'I can't believe I've got to come back here and race.'"

Instead, Earnhardt Jr. tackled it as he does everything in life, with aggression, spirit and enthusiasm. He didn't tremble with fear when he sped through turn four for the first time and he wasn't overcome with emotion when he took the checkered flag.

"I felt OK. I didn't really have any moments that were different or overwhelming," he said. "The very first lap we went around the race track felt different and felt kind of tough. But after the first run we did in practice, it was just like always. I didn't really think much about what happened here in February or anything else.

"We started the race, and I was more nervous about how good my car was than anything else."

There was no need to be. After two days of strong showings in practice, Earnhardt Jr. was the class of the field and as dominant as his father once was at Daytona.

He darted into the lead for the first time on lap 27 and never looked back, leading 116 of 160 laps. His red and white Chevy was so dominant, it shocked nearly everyone, including himself.

"We had such a fast car we could do whatever I wanted with it," he said. "I had the best car here, and everybody saw that."

The question is how and why? Not even Junior and his crew could explain that, another mystery in the strange tale. They tested a faster car, one the crew preferred, but Junior insisted on returning to Daytona with the same car that finished second in the 500.

"The car was just flying," he said. "I can't tell you what (the team) did to it, it was just faster than everybody else's.

"I don't know. Every once in a while you will have a car that will do that, you'll have a car that will be that dominant. Why? We don't know. It just happens."

"When we unloaded, the car was awesome," crew chief Tony Eury Sr. said. "It seemed like anything we did to it, it didn't even bother it. It was just fast for some reason. Some days you hit that and some days you don't."

The only mystery remaining was whether Junior could survive the weird idiosyncrasies of the aerodynamic draft and the inevitable mad dash to the finish.

He faced his only challenge when a multicar wreck on lap 142 shuffled the field, putting Benson, Dave Blaney and others who had pitted before the crash at the front of the field. Junior, who pitted during the caution period, was sixth with just six laps remaining.

But with a dominant car he quickly charged back to the front, and when the wild scramble developed as expected, shuffling Blaney and others backward, Earnhardt Jr. blasted by Benson and into the lead in the space of two laps.

When he saw Waltrip, his teammate and friend, appear in his rearview mirror, he knew he was home free. He had, after all, pushed Waltrip to victory five months earlier.

"To see Michael pull up was cool," he said. "I just knew that he was going to help me, and that's all I needed, just somebody to stay behind me. I knew he wasn't going to move, because I helped him in the 500 and I told him I helped him, so he owed me."

"He called me Monday morning after the Daytona 500 and the first thing he said was, 'I was committed to you, buddy,'" Waltrip recalled. "Those words kept going through my mind all night long. I was committed to him ... and at the end of the race, I pushed him home."

Home to a dream-like, storybook ending that many anticipated, but one that Junior never fathomed.

"I will probably never really get to enjoy this, because I just can't believe it happened," he said.

"I can't understand it. It makes no sense to me. I can't believe it is happening to me, I don't know why it is happening to me. I'm just going to stay close to my friends and the people who make me feel good and maybe someday I will figure it out."

By Jeff Owens

Dale Jr.'s crew erupts as their driver takes the checkered flag.

2001 Pepsi 400 Top Ten

Finish	Start	No.	Driver	Team/Owner	Laps	Money
1	13	8	Dale Earnhardt, Jr.	Dale Earnhardt Inc.	160	$185,873
2	22	15	Michael Waltrip	Dale Earnhardt Inc.	160	108,850
3	38	21	Elliott Sadler	Wood Bros. Racing	160	112,610
4	2	22	Ward Burton	Bill Davis Racing	160	123,285
5	33	18	Bobby Labonte	Joe Gibbs Racing	160	127,777
6	40	25	Jerry Nadeau	Hendrick Motorsports	160	74,425
7	24	2	Rusty Wallace	Penske Racing South	160	102,105
8	30	99	Jeff Burton	Roush Racing	160	103,521
9	43	11	Brett Bodine	Brett Bodine Racing	160	68,725
10	42	7	Mike Wallace	Ultra Motorsports	160	80,286

Time of Race: 2 hours, 32 minutes, 17 seconds
Pole Winner: Sterling Marlin – 183.778 mph
Average Speed: 157.601 mph
Cautions: 3 for 15 laps
Margin of Victory: 0.123 second
Attendance: 168,000

25

Silver Fox's Slickest Move

With A Little Trickery, Pearson Edges Petty

David Pearson was nicknamed "The Silver Fox" for good reason. He was a sly driver who would bide his time until the right strategic move was needed. In the 1974 Firecracker 400, that move turned out to be one that flummoxed the great Richard Petty. Pearson was leading the closing laps, but in the high-speed draft, that's not where he wanted to be. Running second, and being able to utilize the "slingshot" pass, was much better. As he and Petty came down the frontstretch to start the last lap, Pearson let off the gas and turned slightly to the left. Petty thought Pearson was out of gas. Wrong. Pearson tucked into second place and then whipped around Petty over the last thousand yards to win. Petty was NOT amused.

—Steve Waid

Richard Petty was the undisputed king of stock car racing, and he didn't like being embarrassed.

By 1974, Petty had already won more than 100 Grand National/Winston Cup races and four championships. He had won the Daytona 500 four times and would add a fifth at the start of the 1974 season.

At the height of his career, Petty ruled the stock car racing world. He won the most races, was always the championship favorite and owned Daytona, NASCAR's most famous track.

Until July, that is.

In July at Daytona, David Pearson was king, beating Petty in both 1972 and 1973.

The July race at Daytona had carved its own special place in NASCAR history and would go on to become a landmark event, one in which Petty would make history in front of a sitting president 10 years later.

But in 1974, he wanted to win the Firecracker 400 in the worst way, and he wanted to beat Pearson to do it. So much so that he sent a message to his chief rival before the race.

The field is set.
DOZIER MOBLEY PHOTO

"One of the boys in Petty's crew came up to me and said, 'Richard says to tell you that he ain't gonna be embarrassed again,'" Pearson revealed.

But David Pearson, who would go on to win more than 100 races himself, wasn't one to be embarrassed often himself. In fact, he was The Silver Fox, a sneaky, cunning racer prone to pulling off surprising and bewildering victories that embarrassed his competition.

And nothing pleased Pearson more than beating Petty, the undisputed king, and beating him at Daytona, Petty's

David Pearson used some trickery to get to victory lane. They don't call him The Silver Fox for nothing.

1974 Firecracker 400 Top Ten

Finish	Start	No.	Driver	Team/Owner	Laps	Money
1	1	21	David Pearson	Wood Brothers	160	$17,350
2	6	43	Richard Petty	Petty Enterprises	160	12,825
3	5	15	Buddy Baker	Bud Moore	160	12,237
TIE	8	11	Cale Yarborough	Junior Johnson	160	12,187
5	2	16	Bobby Allison	Roger Penske	159	4,100
6	7	28	Bobby Isaac	Hoss Ellington	159	1,900
7	19	54	Lennie Pond	Ronnie Elder	158	3,450
8	29	93	Jackie Rogers	Ray Frederick	157	2,200
9	23	05	David Sisco	David Sisco	155	2,625
10	32	24	Cecil Gordon	Cecil Gordon	153	2,000

Time of Race: 2 hours, 53 minutes, 32 seconds
Pole Winner: David Pearson — 180.759 mph
Average Speed: 138.310 mph
Cautions: 6 for 41 laps
Margin of Victory: 1 car length
Attendance: 65,000

own personal playground.

While he wouldn't win the Daytona 500 for two more years, Pearson owned the Firecracker 400 in 1972-73. His mission in 1974 was to make it three straight.

He accomplished the feat, but to do it, he had to pull a fast one on Petty, snookering him on the final lap and leaving the king once again embarrassed. And, this time, angry.

Pearson had led most of the race, the first event of the year to go its full distance because of the nation's fuel shortage. But for most of the race, Petty was right on his bumper.

Normally, being in the lead at Daytona is the place to be. But not in 1974, when unrestricted engines and boxy cars led to the infamous slingshot move.

"The place to be on the last lap is running second, just behind the leader," Pearson explained. "This makes the leader real vulnerable for the following driver to use aerodynamics – the slingshot technique – to regain the lead with time running out."

With Petty's No. 43 looming in his rearview mirror, Pearson knew he was in the wrong place as he took the white flag. Fearing that Petty was setting him up for a last-lap pass, he took matters into his own hands.

After taking the white flag, Pearson suddenly slowed just past the tri-oval and pulled into the low groove. Petty, taking evasive action, swerved to miss him, then sped away with the lead.

For a moment, it looked as if Pearson, the sly "fox," had fallen victim to a mechanical problem. Instead, he suddenly stomped his accelerator and began to gain on Petty.

Though nearly two seconds and 200 yards behind, Pearson ran down Petty, catching him in the fourth turn. To Petty's shock and dismay, Pearson shot to his inside, regaining the lead and taking the checkered flag for a third straight Firecracker victory.

Petty had been snookered and embarrassed again. Afterwards, he was furious with Pearson.

"I was surprised he backed off so suddenly," Petty said. "David usually drives a safer, saner race. It was a beautiful move as long as he had the faster car and knew he could catch me. If our cars would have been equal, it would have been a stupid move.

"I think it was a mistake on his part to show just how fast his car is. Besides that, we both could have crashed. I was mad because what he did was risky and unnecessary."

Pearson defended himself, saying he did what he had to do to win the race.

"I let Petty go by because I knew he could draft past me as long as he was in second place," Pearson said. "I tried to pull away for about five laps, but I couldn't. So I just acted like my car had quit. I intended for him to think my engine had blown. I didn't think it was a risky move. I pulled to the inside of the track on a straightaway, and I don't think I endangered him."

The move was so slick it fooled his own crew.

"I thought something had gone wrong with the car," said Glen Wood, co-owner of Wood Brothers Racing. "Then we saw David catch up on the backstretch and realized he tricked Petty."

"David was just so smooth. He made it look easy," crew chief and co-owner Leonard Wood said. "He knew exactly what he could do with a car and when he could do it. And before you'd know it, he'd run you into the ground."

Petty, though, was neither impressed nor amused. Still incensed nearly an hour after the race, he came to the press box to confront Pearson.

Though cordial and polite, he made his feelings known during a dramatic, public exchange.

"It was real, real lucky I missed you and didn't crash both of us. It was close," he said to Pearson. "It was a dangerous move. It scared me. You didn't

need to do it. There's no way I could have won the race. You were much faster than me."

"Notice where I did it," Pearson replied to Petty. "I made sure we were out of the dogleg and heading straight. Where I did it, it wasn't a risky move. Faster? I had tried to run off, and I couldn't leave you. But you never would pass me, so I got all the way off the throttle. I knew I had to be second on the last lap to have a chance to win. I couldn't have won if I had stayed in front."

Pearson soon ended the conversation, but Petty stuck around to continue his point.

"If I wanted to be a bad guy, I could have run him into the grass as we came to the flag," Petty said. "But I left him in the lower lane, not the apron, a racing lane. I tried to take up as much room as possible and still be sanitary. If I hadn't, our cars could have crashed and we'd have been in real trouble."

Though trying hard to contain his anger, Petty was clearly rattled and embarrassed.

"It's no big deal to be outrun," he said. "I'm not trying to persecute anyone, but a deal like this upsets you."

It was such cunning, such an unflappable demeanor that led Pearson to 105 career victories. Though widely praised for outsmarting the competition and pulling such a slick move, he downplayed it in typical, modest fashion.

"The way I figured it, there wasn't any gamble to it," he said. "I was going to finish second either way. Might as well give it a try." 🏁

By Jeff Owens (2004)

1980 World 600

Charlotte Motor Speedway
Charlotte, North Carolina
May 25, 1980

Benny Wins The World
Parsons Runs A Super Race

> Benny Parsons and Darrell Waltrip swapped the lead six times during the final 26 laps, and their intense battle had the crowd on its feet. On the next-to-last lap, Parsons got around Waltrip to win by a half-car length in one of the greatest races ever run in Charlotte.
>
> **—Steve Waid**

Benny Parsons, the mild-mannered Grand National driver from Ellerbe, N.C., withstood a furious assault by Darrell Waltrip to narrowly win the rain-plagued World 600 at Charlotte Motor Speedway.

Parsons staged an exciting dash to the finish. He swapped the lead with Waltrip five times over the final 25 laps, finally passing him low in the third turn on lap 398, just two circuits from the conclusion of the 600-mile race. From that point, Parsons valiantly stayed in front of Waltrip to cross the finish line less than a car length in front.

"It was thrilling to be a part of a race that good," said the 38-year-old Parsons. "Today, though, second place would have been hard to take. We needed a victory badly. It might be hard to understand how depressing it is to come so close and still not win. Now we can start thinking about things other than victory."

The Parsons-Waltrip duel began on lap 302, when the green flag fell following the second of two delays caused by rainstorms. When racing began for the final 98 laps, Parsons was the leader over Waltrip, and the two were the only drivers on the same lap.

The duel heated up on lap 375, with Parson passing Waltrip in the fourth turn. The lead changed hands four more times – each bringing resounding cheers from the crowd of 120,000 – before the exciting conclusion.

Parsons' car had to have some chassis adjustments to keep up with the early leaders – Dale Earnhardt and Cale Yarborough. The two drivers clearly had the strongest cars in the field but were eliminated by misfortune.

Because of the rain, the fans who watched the noon start didn't see the finish until 6:40 p.m. There were a record 14 caution flags for 113 laps and 47 lead changes among 12 drivers – another record. Parsons won with an average speed of 119.265 mph, slow for a World 600.

But that does not concern Benny Parsons. What is more important by far is the fact that he won. 🏁

By Steve Waid

DOZIER MOBLEY PHOTO

1980 World 600 Top Five

Finish	Start	No.	Driver	Team/Owner	Laps	Money
1	6	27	Benny Parsons	M G Anderson	400	$44,850
2	7	88	Darrell Waltrip	DiGard	400	38,700
3	11	44	Terry Labonte	Billy Hagan	398	22,660
4	9	43	Richard Petty	Petty Enterprises	397	19,550
5	5	21	Neil Bonnett	Wood Brothers	397	11,250

Time of Race: 5 hours, 1 minute, 51 seconds
Pole Winner: Cale Yarborough – 165.194 mph
Average Speed: 119.265 mph
Cautions: 14 for 113 laps
Margin of Victory: Half car length
Attendance: 120,000

1993 Daytona 500

Daytona International Speedway
Daytona Beach, Florida
February 14, 1993

A 'Different' Dale Scores Daytona Victory

Jarrett Beats Earnhardt For Second Career Win

> It was Dale vs. Dale - Dale Earnhardt against Dale Jarrett. Yep, everyone figured Earnhardt was, at last, going to win the Daytona 500. Nope. Over the last two laps, Jarrett held off Earnhardt's furious charge and won the "big one" for the first time in his career. Jarrett's father, Ned Jarrett, emotionally called the finish from the TV booth.
>
> —Steve Waid

Dale Earnhardt was victimized at Daytona – again. Dale Jarrett, on the final two laps of the 200-lap race, proved he has the skills to match the "Intimidator."

"From my perspective, this is the greatest victory a driver could have," said Jarrett. "I think Dale [Earnhardt] is the best driver to come into racing in a long, long time. He's done everything but win the Daytona 500. You almost have to feel sorry for him."

For Earnhardt, the loss was yet another in what is becoming a long list of Daytona disappointments. For the second time in the last four years, he was the leader as the last lap began.

Following the restart from Rusty Wallace's vicious wreck, the race resumed with Earnhardt at his accustomed position – in front.

Earnhardt stayed in front for 21 consecutive laps, with rookie Jeff Gordon second and Jarrett third.

Once around Gordon and in second place, Jarrett set Earnhardt in his sights as lap 199 came to its end. In the third turn, this time the son of two-time Winston Cup champion Ned Jarrett, who watched his son while serving as a member of the CBS-TV broadcast team, went under Earnhardt – on the low side.

Coming out of the turn, the two Chevrolets bumped. "It was just a slight tap, but Dale was leading and didn't want to give it up," said Jarrett.

Jarrett said he felt confident the win would be his once he was able to squirt ahead out of turn two and maintain his advantage all the way down the backstretch, through the third and fourth turns and into the trioval.

"Dale came on the radio and said, 'It's ours! It's ours!'" said Jarrett's crew chief, Jimmy Makar.

Earnhardt would end up second by 0.16-second, while Geoff Bodine edged Hutt Stricklin for third place.

This victory came in the race called the "Super Bowl of Stock Car Racing," and Joe Gibbs, Jarrett's team owner, coached two Super Bowl winners during his tenure in the NFL.

"Winning the Super Bowl and this race are two great experiences," said Gibbs. "But for this one, I can't take any credit. All I can take credit for is hiring Dale and Jimmy. They put it all together."

Obviously, they did it quite well. 🏁

By Steve Waid

Not a bad way to spend Valentine's Day.
DOZIER MOBLEY

1993 Daytona 500 Top Five

Finish	Start	No.	Driver	Team/Owner	Laps	Money
1	2	18	Dale Jarrett	Joe Gibbs Racing	200	$238,200
2	4	3	Dale Earnhardt	RCR Enterprises	200	181,825
3	6	15	Geoff Bodine	Bud Moore	200	141,450
4	18	27	Hut Stricklin	Junior Johnson	200	95,950
5	3	24	Jeff Gordon	Hendrick Motorsports	200	111,150

Time of Race: 3 hours, 13 minutes, 35 seconds
Pole Winner: Kyle Petty – 189.426 mph
Average Speed: 154.972 mph
Cautions: 7 for 30 laps
Margin of Victory: 0.16 second
Attendance: 135,000

Jarrett's First Winston Cup Win— By Inches

Wood Brothers Claim First Victory Since '87

Dale Jarrett had been a journeyman driver until he earned a ride with the famous Wood Brothers team. At Michigan International Speedway, Jarrett nipped Davey Allison at the finish line by the closest margin in the speedway's history, about 10 inches, to earn his first career win and bring the Woods their first victory since 1987.

—Steve Waid

When the checkered flag fell on the Champion Spark Plug 400, the smiles worn by Dale Jarrett and the Wood Brothers team were larger than the margin of victory Jarrett used to defeat Davey Allison for the first win of his NASCAR Winston Cup career.

Jarrett edged Allison by a scant 10 inches, in one of the closest finishes in history.

"You dream about winning races like that; racing somebody like Davey Allison, to beat somebody like that at the end, race him door to door," Jarrett said with a smile.

With five laps remaining Allison pulled to the outside of Jarrett, and for the last two circuits the two dueled fender to fender. A blown engine in Dave Marcis' Chevrolet on lap 199 didn't result in a caution, and Allison inched ahead as they received the white flag. The two bumped as they raced out of turn two but neither backed off.

Side by side, they raced through turns three and four. Wisps of smoke flew from the cars as they rubbed sheet metal down the frontstretch, but still neither driver cracked the throttle. Neither came close to losing control of his car, and in the photo finish, Jarrett had the win in the palm of his hand.

"I'd done everything I could do aside from wrecking him to try and win," said Jarrett.

"I knew who won the race," Allison said after the race.

"I've been in those situations a couple times before. I have pretty good 'guesstimation' on the car, who's ahead and who's not. This finish was probably the second closest I've ever been in and the second best one I've ever been in. It probably was one of the most fun races I have ever been in."

"I don't like second worth a flip, but if I have to finish second today, it's not too bad doing it to you," said a smiling Allison, who congratulated Jarrett in victory lane, where he held up the Hickory, N.C., driver's hand and then joined him in the winner's interview at the media's request.

For the Wood Brothers, it was the team's first win at MIS since 1978.

One could say the win was Jarrett's going-away gift to the team since he's leaving it at season's end to join a new organization being formed by NFL Washington Redskins coach Joe Gibbs.

By Deb Williams

NS ARCHIVE PHOTO

1991 Champion Spark Plug 400 Top Five

Finish	Start	No.	Driver	Team/Owner	Laps	Money
1	11	21	Dale Jarrett	Wood Brothers	200	$74,150
2	3	28	Davey Allison	Robert Yates Racing	200	47,700
3	9	2	Rusty Wallace	Roger Penske	200	23,600
4	2	6	Mark Martin	Roush Racing	200	30,050
5	4	9	Bill Elliott	Melling Performance	200	26,600

Time of Race: 2 hours, 51 minutes, 34 seconds
Pole Winner: Alan Kulwicki – 173.431 mph
Average Speed: 142.972 mph
Cautions: 4 for 22 laps
Margin of Victory: 10 inches
Attendance: 60,000

After trading the lead—and paint—in the closing laps, Dale Jarrett squeaks by Davey Allison for his first Cup win.

1990 Daytona 500

Daytona International Speedway
Daytona Beach, Florida
February 18, 1990

Cope Victorious In Astonishing Finish

Earnhardt's Cut Tire Paves Way For First Win Of A Young Career

No one could have predicted this. Dale Earnhardt seemed certain to, at last, win the Daytona 500. He was well ahead of Derrike Cope, a relative newcomer. But on the last lap, Earnhardt ran over a broken piece of bell housing and had to back off in the third turn. Cope sped to a victory no one, absolutely no one, thought he had any chance to achieve.

—Steve Waid

Derrike Cope, a NASCAR driver for barely three years, capitalized on the misfortune of a powerful Dale Earnhardt to win the Daytona 500 and thereby earn his first career victory in a stunning upset.

With less than a lap left, Earnhardt, who had made cannon fodder out of the rest of the field throughout the day, suffered a cut tire.

Earnhardt went into the third turn and suddenly drifted high toward the wall. As the astonished crowd looked on, his crippled car was quickly passed by Cope and several other contenders.

"Not in my wildest dreams did I think I could come here and win this race," said Cope.

But until fate lent a hand, Cope was no better than a runnerup. Earnhardt led 155 of 200 laps. Running away from his competition and without benefit of the high-speed draft, Earnhardt cranked out a lead that, with just 20 laps remaining, was nearly 30 seconds ahead of Cope – or more than half a lap.

"There was no way I was going to run Dale down. He had been so tough in the corners. I was just hanging on.

"But then in turn three, I heard a noise and saw some stuff come out from under Dale's car," added Cope. "His car got sideways, and he caught it. It's a tribute to him that he did. It just sort of slid up the track and stopped."

It turned out that it was a piece of a bell housing that Earnhardt had run over in the second turn.

"I knew the right-rear tire was going down on the backstretch," said Earnhardt, who lost the 1986 Daytona 500 to Geoff Bodine when he ran out of gas in the closing laps. "I tried to ride it out. It finally shredded, and then I had all I could handle keeping it off the wall.

"Derrike won the race but I outran everyone all day. He didn't beat us. He lucked into it."

Earnhardt ended up in fifth place. 🏁

By Steve Waid

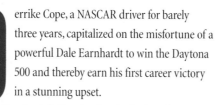

In an astonishing finish, Derrike Cope wins the Daytona 500 and celebrates with his team.
DOZIER MOBLEY PHOTO

1990 Daytona 500 Top Five

Finish	Start	No.	Driver	Team/Owner	Laps	Money
1	12	10	Derrike Cope	Bob Whitcomb	200	$188,150
2	20	1	Terry Labonte	Precision Products	200	117,800
3	4	9	Bill Elliott	Harry Melling	200	114,100
4	19	5	Ricky Rudd	Hendrick Motorsports	200	77,050
5	2	3	Dale Earnhardt	RCR Enterprises	200	109,325

Time of Race: 3 hours, 0 minutes, 59 seconds
Pole Winner: Ken Schrader – 196.515 mph
Average Speed: 165.761 mph
Cautions: 3 for 15 laps
Margin of Victory: 1.5 car lengths
Attendance: 150,000

1989 Daytona 500

Daytona International Speedway
Daytona Beach, Florida
February 19, 1989

Waltrip Gambles And Victory Is His—At Last

Running On Fumes, Waltrip Takes Checkered Flag

Despite all his successes, Darrell Waltrip spent 17 years in NASCAR chasing an elusive victory in the Daytona 500. The chase finally ended after Waltrip nursed his fuel to run the final 132.5 miles without stopping to grab the Holy Grail at long last. He ran out of gas as he pulled into victory lane, where he exuberantly yelled, "I won the Daytona 500! I won the Daytona 500!"

—Steve Waid

For years, all that Darrell Waltrip has been dealt by Fate in NASCAR Winston Cup races at Daytona International Speedway has been a backhand to the face. But in this year's Daytona 500, luck was with him.

Waltrip won a nerve-wracking gamble over fuel consumption. The seventh and final caution began on lap 146. The remainder of the field darted into the pits. On lap 147, Waltrip stopped for tires and fuel. He didn't know it at the time, but it would be his final stop.

He covered 132.5 miles of racing on 22 gallons of gas.

"I thought maybe we could catch Kenny [Schrader] and Dale [Earnhardt], but I saw there wasn't any way we were going to do it," said Waltrip's crew chief Jeff Hammond.

"I asked Darrell what he was thinking and he said, 'Let's do it.' After that, we went to plan B. It was ease up on that throttle and draft, draft, draft. We just kept hoping and praying."

On lap 197, Alan Kulwicki surrendered his lead to Waltrip in the second turn when a right-front tire began going down. It was unfortunate for Kulwicki, who maintained he still had gas in his tank.

Waltrip's lead dwindled, but as he went into the third turn on the last lap, it was clear he had enough to win even if he did run out of fuel.

"I think with two laps to go, the fuel pressure bottomed out twice, but then it came back up again," said Waltrip. "I said on the radio that it was gone, but it picked back up again and I could go on. I don't know what happened. Somehow, somebody gave us some fuel."

Waltrip was one of 15 drivers to swap the lead 30 times, tying the Daytona 500 record set in 1974. He won with an average speed of 148.466 mph.

The victory was the 74th of Waltrip's career. There is no doubt it is the sweetest.

"I won the Daytona 500! I won the Daytona 500!" the ecstatic, nearly-delirious Waltrip yelled in victory lane. "Don't lie to me, this is Daytona isn't it? I'm not dreaming, am I? Thank God!"

By Steve Waid

DOZIER MOBLEY PHOTO

1989 Daytona 500 Top Five

Finish	Start	No.	Driver	Team/Owner	Laps	Money
1	2	17	Darrell Waltrip	Hendrick Motorsports	200	$184,900
2	1	25	Ken Schrader	Hendrick Motorsports	200	182,700
3	8	3	Dale Earnhardt	RCR Enterprises	200	95,550
4	10	5	Geoff Bodine	Hendrick Motorsports	200	79,250
5	7	55	Phil Parsons	Jackson Brothers	200	70,325

Time of Race: 3 hours, 22 minutes, 4 seconds
Pole Winner: Ken Schrader — 196.996 mph
Average Speed: 148.466 mph
Cautions: 7 for 30 laps
Margin of Victory: 7.64 seconds
Attendance: 145,000

THUNDER & GLORY

TOP 25 — BY RACE

RACE	WINNER	TRACK
1974 Firecracker 400	David Pearson	Daytona International Speedway
1976 Daytona 500	David Pearson	Daytona International Speedway
1979 Daytona 500	Richard Petty	Daytona International Speedway
1979 Rebel 500	Darrell Waltrip	Darlington Raceway
1981 Talladega 500	Ron Bouchard	Alabama International Motor Speedway
1984 Winston 500	Richard Petty	Daytona International Speedway
1984 Firecracker 400	Cale Yarborough	Alabama International Motor Speedway
1985 Winston 500	Bill Elliott	Darlington Raceway
1985 Southern 500	Bill Elliott	Alabama International Motor Speedway
1986 Miller 400	Kyle Petty	Richmond Fairgrounds Raceway
1987 The Winston	Dale Earnhardt	Charlotte Motor Speedway
1988 Daytona 500	Bobby Allison	Daytona International Speedway
1991 Goody's 500	Harry Gant	Martinsville Speedway
1992 Hooters 500	Bill Elliott	Atlanta Motor Speedway
1992 The Winston	Davey Allison	Charlotte Motor Speedway
1994 Brickyard 400	Jeff Gordon	Indianapolis Motor Speedway
1995 Goody's 500	Terry Labonte	Bristol Motor Speedway
1997 Southern 500	Jeff Gordon	Darlington Raceway
1998 Daytona 500	Dale Earnhardt	Daytona International Speedway
1999 Goody's 500	Dale Earnhardt	Bristol Motor Speedway
2000 Winston 500	Dale Earnhardt	Talladega Superspeedway
2001 Cracker Barrel 500	Kevin Harvick	Atlanta Motor Speedway
2001 Daytona 500	Michael Waltrip	Daytona International Speedway
2001 Pepsi 400	Dale Earnhardt Jr.	Daytona International Speedway
2003 Carolina Dodge 400	Ricky Craven	Darlington Raceway

THUNDER & GLORY

TOP 25 — BY WINNER

WINNER	RACE	TRACK
Bill Elliott	1985 Winston 500	Darlington Raceway
Bill Elliott	1985 Southern 500	Alabama International Motor Speedway
Bill Elliott	1992 Hooters 500	Atlanta Motor Speedway
Bobby Allison	1988 Daytona 500	Daytona International Speedway
Cale Yarborough	1984 Winston 500	Alabama International Motor Speedway
Dale Earnhardt	1987 The Winston	Charlotte Motor Speedway
Dale Earnhardt	1998 Daytona 500	Daytona International Speedway
Dale Earnhardt	1999 Goody's 500	Bristol Motor Speedway
Dale Earnhardt	2000 Winston 500	Talladega Superspeedway
Dale Earnhardt Jr.	2001 Pepsi 400	Daytona International Speedway
Darrell Waltrip	1979 Rebel 500	Darlington Raceway
Davey Allison	1992 The Winston	Charlotte Motor Speedway
David Pearson	1974 Firecracker 400	Daytona International Speedway
David Pearson	1976 Daytona 500	Daytona International Speedway
Harry Gant	1991 Goody's 500	Martinsville Speedway
Jeff Gordon	1994 Brickyard	Indianapolis Motor Speedway
Jeff Gordon	1997 Southern 500	Darlington Raceway
Kevin Harvick	2001 Cracker Barrel 500	Atlanta Motor Speedway
Kyle Petty	1986 Miller 400	Richmond Fairgrounds Raceway
Michael Waltrip	2001 Daytona 500	Daytona International Speedway
Richard Petty	1979 Daytona 500	Daytona International Speedway
Richard Petty	1984 Firecracker 400	Daytona International Speedway
Ricky Craven	2003 Carolina Dodge 400	Darlington Raceway
Ron Bouchard	1981 Talladega 500	Alabama International Motor Speedway
Terry Labonte	1995 Goody's 500	Bristol Motor Speedway

THUNDER & GLORY

TOP 25 — BY TRACK

TRACK	RACE	WINNER
Alabama International Motor Speedway	1981 Talladega 500	Ron Bouchard
Alabama International Motor Speedway	1984 Winston 500	Cale Yarborough
Alabama International Motor Speedway	1985 Winston 500	Bill Elliott
Talladega Superspeedway*	2000 Winston 500	Dale Earnhardt
Atlanta Motor Speedway	1992 Hooters 500	Bill Elliott
Atlanta Motor Speedway	2001 Cracker Barrel 500	Kevin Harvick
Bristol Motor Speedway	1995 Goody's 500	Terry Labonte
Bristol Motor Speedway	1999 Goody's 500	Dale Earnhardt
Charlotte Motor Speedway	1987 The Winston	Dale Earnhardt
Charlotte Motor Speedway	1992 The Winston	Davey Allison
Darlington Raceway	1979 Rebel 500	Darrell Waltrip
Darlington Raceway	1985 Southern 500	Bill Elliott
Darlington Raceway	1997 Southern 500	Jeff Gordon
Darlington Raceway	2003 Carolina Dodge 400	Ricky Craven
Daytona International Speedway	1974 Firecracker 400	David Pearson
Daytona International Speedway	1976 Daytona 500	David Pearson
Daytona International Speedway	1979 Daytona 500	Richard Petty
Daytona International Speedway	1984 Firecracker 400	Richard Petty
Daytona International Speedway	1988 Daytona 500	Bobby Allison
Daytona International Speedway	1998 Daytona 500	Dale Earnhardt
Daytona International Speedway	2001 Daytona 500	Michael Waltrip
Daytona International Speedway	2001 Pepsi 400	Dale Earnhardt Jr.
Indianapolis Motor Speedway	1994 Brickyard 400	Jeff Gordon
Martinsville Speedway	1991 Goody's 500	Harry Gant
Richmond Fairgrounds Raceway	1986 Miller 400	Kyle Petty

*Formerly Alabama International Motor Speedway